Praise for *Every*

"Life is an intimate embrace in which all things [...]
In *Everyday Oracles*, Ann Bolinger-McQuade [...]
awakened presence in its many signs, colors, and voices. It is a privilege to walk together
on the path of her journey, and awaken to the power and gentleness of the mind with its
dreams and visions. Take this walk and you will find beauty appearing all around you, and
a new sense of discovery within."

—Dr. David N. Russell, Ph.D., D.Sc., author of *Healthy Solutions:
A Guide to Simple Healing and Healthy Wisdom*

"Ann Bolinger-McQuade is a divine messenger. Her book shows us the interconnectedness of all beings. She helps us find the magic of our personal oracles and shows us how to
live happier, more inspired lives. A must read."

—Tina Powers, psychic medium and author of *Reporting for the Other Side*

"Ann Bolinger-McQuade's book is so important because our culture has lost the ability to
interpret personal oracles that can be seen and found everywhere, especially in nature.
Everyday Oracles reminds us that we are part of a living world that speaks to us unceasingly, if we but learn to see and listen."   —Lisa Thiel, visionary artist, singer, and songwriter

"If you found *Everyday Oracles* or it found you, then pick it up and read it. You will walk
away with some kind of message that speaks to you."

—Liza M. Wiemer, author of *Extraordinary Guidance:
How to Connect with Your Spiritual Guides*

"Synchronicities and premonitions are part of our spiritual interconnectedness, and Ann
Bolinger-McQuade describes in brilliant fashion how we can all attune ourselves to the
spiritual life messages laid before us. The question is: Are you willing to hear the message?"

—Shawn A. Tassone, M.D., author of *Spiritual Pregnancy:
Nine Months of Spiritual Transformation Before You Give Birth*

"*Everyday Oracles* connects on so many levels and, in the end, leaves you feeling positive
and hopeful. It is more than the power of positive thinking. It is the power of love that is
sustaining and renewing to the spirit, as food and drink are to the physical body. You are
hard put not to seek such sustenance in your own life. Those who read this book will realize that the universe has indeed given them a gift."

—Elizabeth K. Julian, J.D., former Regional Director,
U.S. Department of Housing and Urban Development

"Here is a down-to-earth guide to leading a magical life."

—Joan Wulfsohn, author of *Stalking Carlos Castaneda*

"*Everyday Oracles* is a captivating story of one woman's divine experience interwoven
with jewels of enlightened messages that everyone can relate to. It will leave you with a
renewed faith in life's possibilities."   —Lisa M. Hopper, author of *In the Wake of a Dream*

"In *Everyday Oracles*, Ann Bolinger-McQuade shares her language of the soul and teaches us to look with new eyes at the miracles that surround us. This book is truly a gift— one to be read and passed on."

—Donna Fontanarose Rabuck, Ph.D., Director, Center for the Sacred Feminine

"Filled with inspiring, real-life stories of individuals who have had their eyes opened to the splendor of what Carl Jung called 'synchronicity.'... If you want to open your eyes, ears, heart, and mind to the many divine voices of Nature around you, this is a good place to start."

—Allan J. Hamilton, M.D., author of *The Scalpel and the Soul* and *Zen Mind, Zen Horse*

Everyday
Oracles

Everyday

Oracles

DECODING THE DIVINE MESSAGES

THAT ARE ALL AROUND US

Ann Bolinger-McQuade

JEREMY P. TARCHER/PENGUIN
a member of Penguin Group (USA) Inc.
New York

JEREMY P. TARCHER/PENGUIN
Published by the Penguin Group
Penguin Group (USA) Inc., 375 Hudson Street,
New York, New York 10014, USA

USA · Canada · UK · Ireland · Australia
New Zealand · India · South Africa · China

Penguin Books Ltd, Registered Offices:
80 Strand, London WC2R ORL, England
For more information about the Penguin Group visit penguin.com

Labyrinth song: Donna Rabuck, Ph.D., with thanks to Cindy Leespring

Most Tarcher/Penguin books are available at special quantity discounts for bulk
purchase for sales promotions, premiums, fund-raising, and educational needs. Special
books or book excerpts also can be created to fit specific needs. For details, write Penguin
Group (USA) Inc. Special Markets, 375 Hudson Street, New York, NY 10014.

Library of Congress Cataloging-in-Publication Data
Bolinger-McQuade, Ann.
Everyday oracles : decoding the divine messages that are all around us / Ann
Bolinger-McQuade.
pages   cm
Includes bibliographical references.
ISBN 978-1-58542-930-1
1. Oracles.   I. Title.
BF1773.B65   2013   2013009655
133.3'248—dc23

Printed in the United States of America
1   3   5   7   9   10   8   6   4   2

BOOK DESIGN BY AMANDA DEWEY

While the author has made every effort to provide accurate telephone numbers, Internet
addresses, and other contact information at the time of publication, neither the publisher
nor the author assumes any responsibility for errors, or for changes that occur after
publication. Further, publisher does not have any control over and does not assume
any responsibility for author or third-party websites or their content.

*Penguin is committed to publishing works of quality and integrity.
In that spirit, we are proud to offer this book to our readers;
however, the story, the experiences, and the words
are the author's alone.*

Some names and identifying characteristics have been changed.

ALWAYS LEARNING   PEARSON

To . . .

. . . the divine mystery that guides and supports us every step of the way.

. . . our ancestors who continue to dance this dream with us.

. . . Rusty, for scouting ahead and returning to let us know it is safe to travel beyond the veil of mystery into the unknown.

. . . my father, who encouraged me to notice and embrace the mysterious world that exists beyond the limits of conventional reality.

. . . and to Kenneth, the love of my life, for his unwavering support, for taking this amazing journey with me and making the life we share beautiful beyond my dreams.

Contents

PART III
Life-Altering Personal Oracles and Amazing Stories

PART I

Personal Oracles Are Everywhere

Chapter 1

Personal Oracles
Portals into Hidden Dimensions

The plants, rocks, fire, water are all alive.
They watch us and see our needs.
They see when we have nothing to protect us and it
is then they reveal themselves and speak to us.

—OLD APACHE STORYTELLER

I was following the precise paper trail my father had created before he passed. In his well-ordered way, Earl had taken care of every detail ahead of time. The small stack of folders on my desk contained the names and phone numbers of everyone I needed to contact. I'd been making phone calls for the past hour, steadily working my way down the to-dos. My next call was to the funeral home in Kansas to arrange for my father's final trip from Tucson to his birthplace. Halfway through dialing, I felt a strong urge to stop. Puzzled, I returned the receiver to its cradle.

The next thought that flashed through my mind was to go

outside and find my husband, Kenneth, who was washing the car in the driveway. In a strange way, it felt like Kenneth had something to share with me. *Well,* I thought, *I might as well stretch my legs and give Kenneth an update on how things are going.*

When I opened the back door, I couldn't believe the feeling that washed over me. From head to toe I felt my father's energy. It was as if he stood next to me, close enough to touch, talk to, laugh with, or go off together on our morning walk. I looked at Kenneth hosing down the car, oblivious to my presence. I walked toward him, and my gaze pulled upward to the clear blue Arizona sky. That's when I spotted it—the image of my father's face in a lone cloud hovering directly above the driveway. I pointed to the sky and called out, "Kenneth, look! It's Daddy!"

He jumped, startled by my voice, then followed the direction of my outstretched arm. He seemed to recognize his father-in-law as naturally as if Earl were washing the car alongside him. Kenneth called back, "That's amazing! He even has his beard."

I explained how I had felt his presence the moment I opened the back door, even before I saw the cloud. "Can you feel it, too?"

Kenneth paused for a moment, then said, "I think I do!"

My father's profile remained in place, its shape unchanging. I needed to catch it on film. I turned toward the house, and a brilliant rainbow spark in the west, opposite my father's cloud presence, caught my eye. Hope filled my heart. I dashed inside, darted up two flights of stairs to my office, and grabbed my camera, all the while laughing and calling out to my father, "Daddy, please wait. . . . Daddy, please wait." And he did.

That treasured cloud photo still hangs in my office, surrounded by a montage of my father's spirit in cloud form that I've captured on film over the years.

In retrospect, I'm not surprised my father's spirit emanates through clouds. Like our Native American ancestors before us, my family lived in a world of metaphor and emerging shapes. For my father, shape recognition and identification was as much a part of him as breathing. He could be eating a piece of toast at the kitchen table and with each bite, observe the change in its shape. When an image emerged that caught his attention, he would interrupt the conversation to note that this piece of toast now resembled a tree, a turtle, a train engine, or whatever he saw. Some of my favorite memories involve driving in the car with him. He would call out, gesturing toward the sky, "Ann, look! Look right there!" then describe the image that appeared to him until I could see it, too.

By sharing what he saw, my father not only gave me permission but also encouraged me to notice what others might miss in our shared world. No wonder I felt like there was more—and hoped there was more—to life than most people realize. As a child, I often imagined how exciting it would be if life were like the page in *Highlights* magazine with hidden information nestled obscurely among the clear lines of familiar objects. Little did I know that my journey would introduce me to wondrous dimensions of our universe and a virtual treasure trove of guidance, comfort, protection, transformation, and so much more.

My awareness of what was happening behind the scenes in our interconnected world expanded in the seventies, when I stumbled upon an intriguing study by former CIA interrogations specialist Cleve Backster. On an impulse, Backster attached his polygraph electrodes to a dracaena plant in his office, then watered the plant to see if it responded. Lo and behold, the needle scratched out a graph just as it did when electrodes were attached to a human. Fascinated, Backster picked up a pair of scissors and approached the plant with the intention of pruning it. Again, the needle moved, registering what he interpreted as fear. He wondered what the machine would do if he threatened the plant. As he imagined lighting a match, he noticed something that forever changed his life. The plant didn't wait for him to strike the match. It reacted to his intention, his thoughts. Further research proved to Backster that intention, not action, triggered the plant's response.

The idea that plants could tune in and respond to a human thought made me view them in a new way. Up to this point, plants had seemed like pretty solid, one-dimensional life-forms, all physical with no emotions or spirit. Recognizing this expanded dimension of their being revealed a new perspective of the world. If plants could react to intention, were trees, rocks, fire, water, and clouds responding, as well? Was all living matter interacting, and I just hadn't noticed? The possibilities appeared endless.

Nothing much changed in my life until a few years later, when a high fever kept me bed-bound for the better part of a week. For days, I drifted in and out of consciousness. I recall moving easily through some sort of safe, albeit unfamiliar, conduit while in a dream state. Although I had no real memory of anything that happened along the way, I awoke with the distinct feeling that I had stepped through some sort of portal. It was like someone had pulled back the three-dimensional curtain so I could glimpse the expanded dimensions of our universe busily responding to everyone's needs. It was clear to me that I could not return to my previous limited perception, nor did I want to. By the time I recuperated, I knew my life direction had changed. Yet I wasn't sure exactly how it had changed.

Then in 1986 a breast cancer diagnosis shocked me to my core, and I was confronted with my deep-seated fear of dying. That's when the universe stepped in and allowed me to experience for myself what Chief Seattle said: "There is no death, only a change of worlds."

All of the right people, animals, birds, clouds, and all kinds of mysterious messages started appearing in my life at exactly the right time. Each with a very specific purpose. Some were in physical form, others in the form of spirit. Coincidence? My intuition said no. Nor was it coincidental that songs playing on the radio had lyrics that spoke directly to what was occurring in my life. Sometimes they offered solutions to my problems, other times they offered reassurance and comfort. Events that had always seemed random in nature now had a recognizable purpose and direction. I had an epiphany—the universe was busily responding to my needs! I paid extra attention to what was happening around me. Animal sightings sent me running to resources to learn the spiritual significance each had for me. Hawks, in particular, started showing up at specific times. According to Ted Andrews, author of *Animal Speak*, the hawk "awakens our vision and inspires us to a creative life purpose."

The more I opened myself up to receiving what I intuitively knew was spiritual guidance, the more guidance I received. As these mystical experiences expanded, I noted that within the visible, mundane lines of life that we see, smell, hear, taste, and touch each day lie private messages of guidance, support, protection, reassurance, and insight. These messages, which come in every imaginable form, do not originate in our three-dimensional world. Rather, I'm convinced they come from the realm of Spirit and are delivered right when we need them the most. It's as if a spiritual version of the *Highlights* game is continually playing out all around us—and all we have to do is notice.

I felt like I had stepped onto an invisible moving sidewalk, like the ones that you find in airports, transporting me through a portal into other dimensions of our world. Not only are these dimensions filled with marvelous mysteries, they are spaces abundant with joy, hope, laughter, and guidance, all of which make my life feel more complete and gratifying. I soon realized that I was being charged with the responsibility of quantifying and sharing this perspective of our interconnected universe and its magnificent design. The underlying purpose being to dispel the notion that we are all alone as individuals floating through time and space—ending up in a black hole or earning our way to a literal heaven and hell.

I started thinking about how to describe this amazingly flexible and adaptive mode of communication that exists in our everyday world. At first I called these mysterious occurrences gifts from the universe, because they are, and yet that didn't feel quite right. The gifts I received were tailored specifically to my needs; they were personal. So I coined the term "personal oracles."

What are personal oracles? You know them. They're those mysterious messages that seem to materialize at just the right moment. They may whisper in your ear or engage another one of your senses with a message that says *"Go this way,"* or *"Consider this,"* or even transmit a message from a deceased loved one telling you, *"I'm still here."* They are everyday miracles that can be so minor we barely notice or so large they make us gasp in awe. Personal oracles are the language the universe uses to communicate with us. Just as the teacher at a chalkboard enlarges our world using the letters of the alphabet, personal oracles expand our awareness with their messages. They speak to what's occurring in your life at a particular time. When it comes to personal oracles, there is no "One size fits all." The universe tailors its messages to you. Though the messages you receive are different from the messages I receive, they all originate in the same universal spirit.

In essence, personal oracles are sources of guidance and support that continually flow through everything in the universe. They come to each of us in the form of timely messages that resonate through every form imaginable and illuminate our interconnectedness. These life-affirming messages dissolve, if only for an instant, the illusion that we are separate.

After years of studying the dynamics of personal oracles, working with people on an individual basis, and conducting personal oracle workshops, I know how easy and natural it can be to incorporate their guidance into everyday life. And how rewarding.

PERSONAL ORACLES: ONLY THE NAME IS NEW

Personal oracles have been around for as long as people have inhabited this planet. Almost every religion and culture through-out history has embraced its own oracle stories and practices. The ancient Babylonians, for example, looked to the clouds for oracle messages. Nephomancy, or cloud gazing, is one of the oldest and most widely used forms of divination in the world. The Druids used it extensively, calling it by the Celtic term *neladoracht*. Also in the Western world were the ancient Greeks, who still retain a reputation for being oracle aficionados. For them, oracles were wellsprings of divination and prophecy available to all citizens, from the common worker to kings, philosophers, and religious leaders. Oracles addressed personal issues, politics, philosophy, religions, law, social mores—no topic was taboo.

At the Oracle of Zeus at Dodona, messages were conveyed to priests and priestesses via the rustling leaves of a sacred oak tree. At the Oracle of Apollo at Delphi, seekers brought their questions to a high priestess who would receive information from Apollo and relay it in a foreign-sounding garble to priests capable of interpreting the message. This oracle, purported to be the most influential of all in Greece, played a major role in the lives of people still familiar to us, including Socrates, who took one particular personal oracle to heart.

When Socrates was about thirty years old, well before he became famous as a philosopher, his friend Chaerephon visited the Oracle at Delphi and asked, "Is there a man alive wiser than Socrates?" The high priestess answered, "No, there is no one wiser than Socrates." When Socrates heard this, he set out on a mission to test and understand the oracle's pronouncement. He began by seeking out people reputed to be wise, then testing their knowledge through questioning. What he discovered was a good deal of inflated ego, ignorance, and false claims to knowledge, but no one with genuine wisdom. Ultimately, Socrates concluded that the oracle was correct. He was the wisest because he recognized his own lack of knowledge while others did not recognize theirs. This method of questioning, called the Socratic method, has been used throughout history and is at the foundation of Socrates Cafés, which now are held around the world. These forums are attended by everyday people who use the Socratic method of questioning and reasoning to explore thoughtful ideas and experiences.

Like the Greeks, Native Americans have recognized and found guidance in everyday personal oracles for thousands of years. In his book *Spirits of the Earth*, Bobby Lake-Thom, a Native American healer, shares an example of how a hawk that appeared in a dream saved his daughter's life. He writes about the night his wife and baby daughter were fast asleep beside him and his wife dreamed she saw a weak baby hawk trying to fly with its mother. But it wasn't able to keep up. The baby hawk started falling to the ground. In her dream, Thom's wife heard the mother hawk say, *"Wake up, sister, wake up. Your baby is in trouble."* The hawk's screams jarred her awake. She immediately discovered that her long hair had gotten wrapped around her infant daughter's throat. Thom cut his wife's hair, and their baby was not injured.

Today in places like the Taos Pueblo, a continuously inhabited settlement in New Mexico that dates back thousands of years, Native Americans live in a way that honors the earth as sacred. They experience their world as alive and imbued with a spirit similar to their own, and rely on spiritual messages to guide them. They offer prayers of gratitude to the Great Mystery for "Mother Earth, Father Sky, the two-legged, the four-legged, the winged ones and all my relations." It is their belief that a person's spirit joins ancestors in the clouds and returns in the form of rain and rainbows to bless the earth and make it fertile. This understanding of the relationships that bind together natural forces and all forms of life has been fundamental to their ability to live for millennia in spiritual and physical harmony with the land.

In 2001, I had the great honor of meeting Richard Deertrack, an elder of the Taos Pueblo. He recognized what I was trying to develop in my work and offered to help me in any way he could. He ended up having a profound effect on my life and my work. He was the missing link that reconnected me with the ancient Native American wisdom that lay dormant in my consciousness.

Like the Native American culture, the Hawaiian culture abounds with personal oracles found in nature. Famed Hawaiian elder Nana Veary, known for her spiritual seekings and writings, described her childhood as "a place where birds, clouds, and stones spoke as clearly as people, because the silent language of nature was profoundly understood." Some Polynesians consider the lizard to have supernatural powers. It's said that when you see a lizard you may actually be looking at the spirit of a dead ancestor. Native American culture associates the lizard with dreaming. It seems that both cultures associate this quick-moving reptile with the ability to move between dimensions.

Personal oracles also extend to the Middle East, where they came in many shapes and sizes, including Moses' tablets with the Ten Commandments, a divine pronouncement received from on high. A more recent oracle occurred in this century. A report about Saudi Arabian prince Abdullah's visit to the United States in 2008 suggests that messages from animals are revered in his culture. Arriving at President George W. Bush's Texas ranch angry about the president's position on Israel and Ramallah, Prince Abdullah quickly decided he wanted to leave. But when he spotted a turkey on the road, he took it as a positive sign from Allah. The prince changed his mind and decided to stay. The report doesn't include details about what the turkey symbolized to the prince. From the way it influenced his decision to stay, it's pretty safe to guess that in the Middle East, as in many cultures around the world, the turkey is a sign of blessings and abundance and an indication that efforts will be rewarded proportionate to one's efforts.

Throughout history, all around the world personal oracles have been speaking to humans every day, through clouds, the Oracle at Delphi, the Ten Commandments, hawks, turkeys, and, as you will soon see, every other form imaginable.

If you were participating in a Socrates Café, you might ask:

"Why do personal oracles happen?"

"What's at work in the universe to make them appear?"

"What the heck is going on here?"

OUR INTERCONNECTED WORLD

In the late 1970s, I participated in a large group meditation in Dallas, where I lived at the time. After the meditation ended, participants shared their experiences. The accounts were dramatic—astral travel to distant galaxies, prophetic messages of various kinds. I remained silent, hesitant to describe my rather simplistic vision of a luminescent web of energy shaped like a giant net.

This concept of an interconnected world is as ancient as the concept of oracles. The Vedas, the oldest scriptures in Hinduism, dating back to 1500 B.C., speak of a unified field of pure consciousness that bathes and permeates all creation. Around 500 B.C., Confucius wrote: "My way is crossed by a single thread that connects everything." Fast-forward to the twentieth century, and you have scientist Max Planck, father of quantum physics, describing a matrix of interconnections that he characterized as the container of the universe. More recently, quantum physicists have proposed the string theory, which contends that the universe consists of tiny vibrating strings of energy, along with ten, eleven, or possibly twenty-six different dimensions.

American naturalist John Muir eloquently summed up our invisible web of life with this statement: "When we try to pick out anything by itself, we find it hitched to everything else in the Universe." Talk about mind-boggling!

Like a safety net constructed purposefully beneath the tightrope walker, the links that connect us with everything in the universe support us, guide us, and keep us secure. In a couple of regions located on opposite sides of the world, not only the

concept but also the words used to describe our inte
ness are surprisingly similar.

Dream weave. In her book *Dancing the D*
American author Jamie Sams describes the dream weave as an "intangible web of life, which is comprised of threads of energy, thought, emotion, intent, ideas, and life force; the connective tissue that exists in our universe as the unseen energetic pathways, forming a web that is connected to all solid matter, all levels of awareness, and all animate and inanimate life forms." Nothing within the dream weave is separate.

Dreamtime. From the Aboriginal culture "down under," the term "dreamtime" is used to describe a complex network of interconnections. Indigenous Australian peoples view all phenomena and life as part of a vast and complex system of relationships that trace back to what they call "the ancestral Totemic Beings of the Dreaming." They believe that each of us exists eternally in the "dreaming" that precedes our birth and continues after we die.

Songlines. Also found within the Australian culture are songlines, described as invisible lines of energy that traverse the earth and link everything associated with it. The image of an expansive web again comes to mind. These lines are activated by song and dance. For nomadic people, these songlines were like compasses. As tribes moved from place to place, singing connected them with the invisible lines of energy that guided their path. Australian Aboriginal elder and keeper of sacred sites Aunt Millie Boyd gave us a glimpse into the tradition of songlines when she offered this blessing to author Anne Wilson Schaef, who was traveling the world gathering information for her book *Native Wisdom for White Minds*: "You have much to do, I will sing you to safety."

Leylines. British leylines provide another culture's take on the infinite web of energy that supports us. Leylines are thought to be magnetic in nature, the same "lines" that birds, mammals, insects, and bacteria use to migrate long distances. Some suggest that leylines follow the cosmic energy of the earth and as such can be dowsed by using a dowsing rod or picking up this energy through one's finely tuned senses. Ancient structures like Stonehenge are thought to be located at the point where two or more leylines intersect.

Vortexes. A vortex is created by spiraling energy that exists where two or more leylines interconnect. These areas of concentrated energy can be found throughout the world and are considered sacred sites. Here, the energy flowing through multiple dimensions is magnified. This energy interacts with each person's body, mind, and spirit in a unique way that can be best understood through firsthand experience. My home state of Arizona has four renowned vortexes in Sedona. I love to spend a few days there, soaking in the positive energy. Each time I drive away, I feel the energy abruptly shift. It's like turning off a light switch of luminescent energy and returning to the more familiar energy of everyday life.

In an attempt to quantify how energy vortexes affect us, scientists have measured biochemical changes that occur when a person spends time within a vortex. They have learned that these centers are heavily charged with negative ions. Negative ions rid the air of pollen, dust, and so on—stuff you can see under a microscope. They also improve a person's mood and can have a positive impact on their health. While we wait for technology to solve the mysteries of vortexes, we can learn much from the ancient ones who understood that everything in the universe emits unseen energy. They understood that we sense it intuitively and logically even if we can't see it, touch it, or taste it. They understood that each person receives and responds to the rhythms of divine energy in their own way.

Okay, it's time to connect some dots. Throughout millennia, people have been talking about invisible energetic pathways that flow through all solid matter, through all animate and inanimate life-forms, and through all levels of awareness. These energy pathways even flow up through the atmosphere to the solar system and back again. The energy lines flow through us, too. In Traditional Chinese Medicine, these lines are called meridians and were charted more than two thousand years ago. Acupuncturists insert needles along meridian points associated with certain diseases. Absolutely everything in our world, solar system, and universe has energy running through it, and this web of energy connects me to you, and you to him, and him to the stream, and the hawk to her, and us to the clouds, and so it goes. It's like the old song "Dry Bones." "The head bone connected to the neck bone, the neck bone connected to the backbone. . . . Oh, hear the word of the Lord."

Here's another way to think of it. Most of us use electrical current every day without giving any thought to the energy to which we're connecting. We turn on our computer, and the monitor comes to life. We turn on the television, hear a sound, and watch images dance across the screen. Personal oracles work the same way. They are energy-driven miracles waiting for us to tune in and notice them. And when we do, voilà, our world changes. It's like in the classic movie The Wizard of Oz. Remember how the movie is in black-and-white until Dorothy lands in Oz and emerges from her house? The world springs to life in full

Technicolor. Daily life can seem a bit bleak without personal oracles to guide us. But when we step through portals into previously hidden dimensions, our everyday life is illuminated by magnificence beyond our wildest dreams. After one of my workshops, a woman sent me this e-mail:

> I've always been afraid to consider spiritual things. I feared what might happen, how it might change my life. But today I heard people share so many great stories that I'm excited to let personal oracles into my life. I'm going to start paying attention to what's out there for me. P.S. I love the idea of being so connected and protected.

Personal oracles add a rich layer of meaning to a world that can seem lonely and devoid of magic or dialogue with the divine. Like a safety net constructed beneath a tightrope walker, personal oracles connect us to everything in our interactive universe that is ready and waiting to support us, guide us, and keep us secure. When you tune in and start connecting the dots for yourself, I guarantee it will change the way you experience life.

Just remember, personal oracles are here for the taking.

Chapter 2

How Personal Oracles Work
Conduits, Mirrors, and More

*My way is crossed by a single thread
that connects everything.*

—CONFUCIUS, CA. 500 B.C.

Let's delve into personal oracles a little further, into their characteristics and the specifics of how they work. What do they look like? Sound like? Feel like? Where can they be found, and how do you know when you're staring yours in the face? If you're thinking the world of personal oracles sounds mysterious and perhaps too challenging to decipher, let me assure you that learning to recognize personal oracles is easy. It's like learning to ride a bike. At first you wobble and have to plant a foot on the ground to stay upright, but with practice your feet remain on the pedals, and you can focus on the surrounding landscape. That's when fascinating details begin to emerge.

PERSONAL ORACLE CATEGORIES

When learning to identify personal oracles, I find it helpful to divide them into five main categories:

- Conduits
- Mirrors
- Synchronicities
- Signs and Symbols
- Invisible Moving Sidewalks

Following are examples of personal oracles within each category. You may want to keep a notebook of what you identify as your personal oracle and the category in which it fits. Since some oracles fit into more than one category, there's no right or wrong way to categorize them. Just the act of doing so helps clarify what's occurring and makes you more cognizant of what's going on behind the scenes. After a while this exercise becomes like training wheels—dispensable. You put the kickstand up and start pedaling through your day, more aware of your personal oracles popping up here and there along the way.

CONDUITS

Think of a conduit as a pipeline or channel through which personal oracles are delivered into your life. Because this pipeline never closes and remains free from obstructions, oracles can pour into your life when you least expect them. The universe is creative when choosing conduits. As you will see in the next three stories, they come in all shapes, sizes, and species.

One of the marvelous things about personal oracles is that you never know where or when they will appear, and how they will help you. Rhonda discovered this when she took her two little dogs, Taz and Toto, for their midday walk near their home in a remote mountain area. She and her dogs had walked the length of their long, winding driveway and were approaching the gravel road when a hummingbird flew toward her. It came to an abrupt halt, hovering a few inches directly in front of Rhonda's face and forcing her to stop in her tracks. Normally she would have dodged the hummingbird and kept right on walking but the word "danger" began flashing in her mind like a vivid neon sign. Prickles of fear coursed up the back of her neck as a sense of urgency to return home shot through her.

Rhonda gathered her two little dogs in her arms, turned on her heel, and broke into a run. As she ran, the word "danger" now became audible and sounded repeatedly in her left ear. It was as if someone was speaking directly to her, yet no one was there. When she glanced back over her shoulder to make sure they were safe, she saw the same hummingbird perched on the branch of a tree. She felt like it was watching her to make sure she was heeding its warning. Once she and her dogs were safely inside, Rhonda noticed her answering machine signaling a message that had not been there when she left the house.

The distressed voice of the neighbor who lived across the dirt road was instructing her to stay inside, alerting her to a pack of wild dogs that were roaming the area. He went on to say the dogs had killed one goat, attacked and seriously injured their sheep-dog as it tried to protect the goats, and brutally killed their dear old family dog that had been napping on the front porch. There had been no doubt about the urgency of the hummingbird's warning, and now Rhonda understood why.

Kenneth and I needed to drive both our cars from New Mexico back to Tucson. He led the way, and I tried not to let too many other cars come between us. About four hours into the trip, I spotted a large heart-shaped cloud with a human-looking face hovering over the highway in front of Kenneth's car. At the same time I became aware of extraordinary feelings of comfort and protection that seemed to fill the car. The sense of protection that permeated the car was as pronounced as the cloud that hovered above the highway.

To my amazement, this cloud did not change its shape as clouds must do, nor did the feelings of protection dissipate. This cloud remained as unwavering as the moon in the sky, and the sense of security surrounding me as strong as a stone fortress. I basked in the feelings of love and protection. Just as I had felt my father's energy coming through a cloud, I knew that these feelings were radiating from the heart cloud. It dawned on me that this cloud was foretelling a safe journey for us. Five minutes passed and the cloud continued to claim its place in the sky in the exact same shape. Fifteen minutes and still it was steadfast. I resisted taking a photo of the cloud while driving, but after twenty minutes, I gave in. With only Kenneth's car in sight, I reached

over for the camera on the passenger seat, popped open the lens, and snapped a few photos of our protector cloud.

An hour or so later, a loud bang came from Kenneth's car and it lurched to the right. The back end swerved and the brake lights flared. I hit my brakes and followed Kenneth as he guided the now unstable car safely onto the shoulder of the road. The right rear tire deflated in less than a blink. I jumped out of my car.

"What did you think of that spectacular heart-shaped cloud?" I said, sure this man who had instantly recognized his father-in-law in a cloud had been in tune with what had just played out. Kenneth looked puzzled. He hadn't seen or felt the cloud and couldn't understand what I was going on about until he saw the photo. Then I realized why. It was my personal oracle.

Other people can be right there and not notice anything. Such is the way of personal oracles.

The reason for the heart cloud was clear: it was a conduit of protection. Spirit had answered my routine request for a safe journey. With heartfelt gratitude, I gave thanks for that protection.

⌐

Alan parked his single-engine Cessna 182. He jumped out of the plane, adjusted his cowboy hat, and headed over to a group of pilots mingling near the office.

"Are you the cloud seeders?" Alan asked.

A couple of the men looked surprised. "I guess word gets around during a drought," said a tall fellow.

"So how does this seeding work?" asked Alan. He owned a large ranch that was suffering from lack of rain. He knew that cloud seeding could initiate rain but had never tried it.

The pilots explained that they would fly up to the base of the cloud to be seeded. At this height of about twelve thousand feet, an updraft would pull moisture into the clouds, causing their tops to billow up and out. To seed them, they shot flares of silver iodide vapor into the cloud base. The vapor would get sucked up into the cloud, and rain would start, often within ten minutes. The vapor also increased the cloud's natural rainfall.

"If you see any clouds floating due east, could you seed them for me?" said Alan. "My ranch is that way and sure could use some rain."

The tall pilot answered. "Would love to help you out, but that's too close to the New Mexico state line. We're federally funded and the law tells us where we can and can't seed."

"But we can tell you how to seed," piped up another pilot.

By the time Alan climbed back in his plane, he was well versed in cloud-seeding techniques and knew where to order the flares. A week later, he was ready to launch project cloud seed. He kept his eyes peeled to the sky, waiting for the right clouds to position themselves in the right place. They finally did, and Alan took off in his plane equipped with flares.

The project proved to be wildly successful. Alan learned that he could seed one cloud and then move on to a second and even a third. But the flying was risky. The turbulence bounced the plane around like a small toy, making it quite a challenge for him to hook the wires to the battery that would shoot the flares attached to brackets under the plane. He prayed he wouldn't get knocked out in the cabin. More than once after seeding, he landed on his ranch's airstrip in two to three inches of water. By the end of the summer, his rain gauges measured fifty percent above normal while ranches thirty or forty miles away in all directions remained dry. Alan didn't mention his cloud-seeding efforts and results to any neighbors. For all he knew, he was breaking every rule and regulation in the book.

One day, clouds filled the horizon and grew fast and large, indicating the air was plump with moisture. It was a perfect day for seeding. Alan drove to the hangar where his plane was ready with flares already bolted into their brackets. As he opened the pickup's door to get out, he heard a voice.

"*Don't fly today.*"

Alan looked around, even though he knew he was alone.

"*Don't fly today.*"

No one was even within shouting range. But the voice was clear and slow.

"Don't fly today," the insistent voice said.

Alan had never experienced anything like this. He knew he had heard the voice. There was no question about what it said. It struck him as more perplexing than frightening. He wanted to seed. The ranch needed the rainfall so he started to argue with the voice out loud.

"But these clouds are so good. It'd be a darn shame not to seed them."

"Don't fly today."

He sat in the pickup for ten minutes trying to figure out what was going on. Something inside tugged at him. He decided that he'd better pay attention to the mysterious admonition. He rationalized that the ranch already had a good amount of rain and was in great shape for the fall, so one day without seeding wouldn't make any difference. He closed the pickup's door and drove the mile back to ranch headquarters.

That afternoon it rained so hard that the Gila, the river running through Alan's ranch, overflowed and flooded the nearby town of Duncan. It washed the elementary school away and three people drowned.

Before the day ended, Alan knew that he had made the right decision. If he had seeded that day, more people might have died. Even if he had lived through flying and landing in a deluge, he would have felt guilty for those three deaths. He concluded that he knew too little about the weather and had been playing God. The warning he received had been so clear, so plain, that he needed to acknowledge it. He felt eternally grateful to the voice that warned him not to fly. From that point on, Alan never seeded another cloud.

Luckily Rhonda recognized the hummingbird working as a

conduit delivering a message. As with Alan, her intuition said to listen to that message and she did. Acting on intuitive feelings without getting caught up in doubt and mind chatter that can pull us off track can keep us, and even others, out of a whole lot of trouble.

MIRRORS

Imagine your world is filled with magical mirrors. Each mirror reflects information back to you to enhance your life. Some mirrors reflect precisely what is going on at the moment. Others work as billboards and spirit signposts to guide our way. If you've seen holograms on exhibit at a museum, you may have moved around them and noticed the way they reflect different images to you. Thinking of the universe in terms of a giant hologram can help us understand how personal oracles are reflected to us according to where we are and what is occurring in our life at the time.

Clouds serve as handy mirrors and offer a never-ending panorama of shapes and images that can reflect special messages back to us. One day, for instance, when I was feeling out of sorts and needed to lighten up, I spotted a cloud in the shape of a human head with its mouth open, as if it were laughing out loud. Just like when someone else's yawn triggers your yawn, this cloud made me giggle and shifted my mood from the shadows to the sunshine. Ever since that day, images of laughing clouds seem to pop up at just the right time.

Another personal oracle that mirrors valuable information to me comes by way of a turtle-shaped boulder that sits high above a road just outside Taos, New Mexico. Each time I pass by I'm reminded of the story of the tortoise and the hare. Remember how the hare darts and dashes around while the tortoise moves steadily along at its own slow and easy pace? Well, we all know who wins the race—and it's not the frenzied hare! The Taos turtle is a gentle reminder to me, an Aries who is astrologically programmed for speed, to slow down and savor the moment.

I was puzzled when a woman at one of my workshops asked for directions to the Taos Turtle Monument. Just so you know, the

Taos turtle is a magnificent boulder tucked neatly into sagebrush high above the road. It is not a monument, but a natural rock formation that can easily be passed by and never noticed.

⌐

Georgia discovered this personal oracle mirror in nature. In need of fresh air and movement, she stepped out of her art studio and headed down the path into the woods. Walking beyond her normal route, she rounded a bend and came face-to-face with a perfectly symmetrical tree. She stood in awe, allowing herself to experience its presence. How perfectly aligned the limbs. How straight and strong the trunk. Its healthy green leaves fluttered in the breeze, twisting and turning like graceful dancers.

Georgia closed her eyes and tuned in to her body, trying to imagine her core as the tree trunk. She noticed tightness in her shoulders, felt it in her locked jaw. She had been feeling confrontational and out of sorts lately, but had no idea so much tension had invaded her body. She inhaled deeply, then exhaled slowly, trying to release the pent-up energy she held in her body. The tension began to drain. Finally, with a bow of respect to the tree, she headed toward home inspired to paint this perfectly aligned tree that so gracefully held the balance she needed in her life.

⌐

This mirror arrived in the form of a fist-bump from a butterfly. I was racing to the airport terminal in my favorite high-heeled boots from the last row of short-term parking when I realized that I wasn't wheezing, much less out of breath. It was a wow moment, especially since a few years earlier my asthma had made walking any distance at that pace out of the question. At that very moment, a butterfly fluttered right in front of me. It was like a fist-bump from a butterfly. The universe was acknowledging the healing transformation of my lungs—from asthma to good health! How did I understand the message from the butterfly? The timing, of course, and remembering that a butterfly, which enters the cocoon as a crawling caterpillar and emerges as winged beauty, is an ancient sign of transformation and renewal.

The following example of a personal oracle being delivered through a mirror came to me via Sandra, a workshop attendee who is a professional intuitive.

> The orange tree outside my kitchen window had a bumper crop of the sweetest, most luscious oranges that I ever had tasted. I was being spoiled and I knew it. So was a beautiful flicker with a crimson head that landed regularly and sipped eagerly from the nectar. It seemed like every time I washed dishes in the sink, he was there. He always landed on the same branch and squealed out his bliss before he poked his beak into the fruit and drank and drank to his heart's delight. This little guy was in ecstasy.
>
> The little flicker visited every day for a couple of months, always landing on the same branch where the oranges were most abundant. The morning after a huge windstorm, I noticed that branch had been stripped clean of fruit. When the flicker landed, I could see his frustration. He cocked his head back and forth as if he was looking at the other branches still full of oranges. But "his" branch

was empty. His beak that had always squealed out enthu-siasm now opened and closed soundlessly in apparent aggravation or bewilderment. He sat there for a long time. It seemed like he was trying to figure out what to do. Finally he flew off and I never saw him again.

The flicker reminded me of the Five of Cups card in a tarot deck. This card shows a person looking at three cups that have spilled. The person looks sad. Two cups, however, remain upright, but the person's back is turned so he can't see them. The flicker reminded me that instead of looking at the empty branch, focus on the oranges that still fill the tree.

It also reminded me of countless readings I've done for people who want change to happen to them, but don't want to initiate the change. I tell them it's like listening to a bad radio station and hoping the music will get better. It won't. You have to take charge and change the station to get the music you want. These individuals could benefit from the personal oracle that was mirrored by this tiny flicker: If you want to feast on the juice of ripe oranges, be willing to move to a new branch.

SYNCHRONICITIES

"Synchronicity" is a term coined by the famed psychologist Carl Jung, who believed in an underlying order to the universe that manifested itself through meaningful coincidences. The term was inspired by an event that occurred during one of Jung's psychotherapy sessions with a patient who was at an impasse with her treatment. The previous night, this woman had dreamed of a golden scarab beetle. During the session the next day, an insect smashed into Jung's cabinet. He caught it and discovered, to his surprise, that it was a golden scarab, a very rare insect in that climate. The significance wasn't merely the coincidental appearance of the hard-shelled creature following the patient's dream. Jung knew it had a deeper meaning. From his knowledge of ancient esoteric philosophies, he knew that the golden scarab beetle symbolized encouragement and the ability to overcome hurdles. He knew that his patient would move past her obstacles with flying colors.

So you might think of synchronicities as coincidences with a purpose. Like all personal oracles, they guide us, deliver information when we most need it, and in the process illuminate the interconnectedness of all. If you take a moment, you might even recall some synchronicities that have played out in your life. If not, here are examples to jog your memory.

Jackie was writing a scene for her novel when she hit a missing fact. She needed to know the name of a particular famous Brazilian soccer player. She thought it was Ronaldo, but for some reason she thought there was more than one Ronaldo. She opted to keep writing and Google later. After an hour, she headed to the kitchen to refill her coffee cup. *The Wall Street Journal* lay on the counter near the coffeemaker. Not quite ready to sit down again, she started paging through it. Her eye landed on the headline "Know Your Ronaldos." She couldn't believe it. The short article consisted of photographs and brief bios of three soccer players:

Cristiano Ronaldo, the Portuguese native who played soccer in England; Ronaldo, the Brazilian striker considered "the best goal-scorer on the planet"; and Ronaldinho, the Brazilian mid-fielder. It was precisely the information she needed.

Some people might call this chance happening a coincidence, one of those remarkable sequences of events that seem to have no relation to each other. Yet when we look through the paradigm of personal oracles, we notice interconnected threads of energy in action. It results in serendipity. Author and mythologist Joseph Campbell defined serendipity as "a thousand unseen helping hands," bringing to fruition what is meant to be but is totally unexpected. You also might call such an event a synchronicity.

⟶

Nancy was still reeling from her husband's diagnosis of AML, a rare form of leukemia, when she answered her front door and the cheerful face of a seven-year-old boy was looking up at her. She glanced down at the piece of paper in his hands and wondered which summer camp he was selling candy for. As it turned out he wasn't selling candy for camp at all. He was collecting donations for AML research. The little guy smiled when he told Nancy that he had had AML since he was two, and then he announced proudly that a transplant had saved his life. She wanted to grab him and hug him but instead she wrote out a check with gratitude for the rays of hope that were returning.

Some synchronicities can save our bacon, as happened to this woman. While speeding along an open stretch of road, her mind preoccupied with what she wanted to get done before she picked up her daughter at school, a license plate caught her attention. The woman touched the brake and slowed down to get a closer look at the letters—GVT. She was pondering the significance of the abbreviation for "government" when, out of the corner of her eye, she noticed a speed camera. Her heart skipped a beat before she realized the hidden significance of the license plate. It had just kept her from getting a speeding ticket!

Other synchronicities make us aware, after the fact, of how interconnected everything is. Hollis was cruising along the open road at ninety miles per hour. A truck approaching in the other lane began blinking its headlights wildly, so Hollis slowed down, acknowledging the universal alert signal for "You are about to encounter a speed trap!" Moments later, now traveling a respectable seventy-five miles per hour, Hollis passed a county sheriff. As he looked in his rearview mirror to confirm that the sheriff remained parked alongside the road, Hollis registered on the synchronicity of the song playing on the radio. It was Alison Krauss singing "The Lucky One."

Synchronicities reveal the presence of a helping hand in myriad ways. Dr. Donna Rabuck was preparing for a presentation but couldn't locate a specific piece of information. She picked up a bulging file, ready to dig through it. Before she even set the file on the desk, one piece of paper slipped out. It was the exact information she needed. "This kind of thing happens to me all the time," she told me. "It's like the information I need jumps right out in front of me."

Here's another instance of needed information coming in right on cue. My friend Tom was a newly appointed CEO of a local bank, charged with the formidable task of assembling a new team to pull the company out of the slump created by the mortgage crash of 2008. One candidate for a high-level position stood out above the others. After numerous interviews and long negotiations, the prospective employee, John, accepted the position and left, prepared to submit his two weeks' notice to his current employer. The next day Tom's intercom buzzed. "John is on line one." He picked up the phone expecting nothing but good news. "What can I do for you, John?" There was a long pause, then John explained that when he turned in his resignation, the company sweetened the pot, and he had decided to stay where he was.

Back to square one, Tom thought as he hung up the phone. A file that had been sitting on the corner of his desk throughout the entire interview process caught his eye. "Catherine Newbury," it said on the tab. A sharp woman with an impressive background, she had been a tempting choice to fill the position all along, but John had edged her out because he had been with his company longer. Just the thought of hiring her filled him with a sense of calm and purpose.

Indeed, Catherine turned out to be a key planner in the bank's turnaround. She had strong connections in the community and generated more new business than anyone could have projected. She was the perfect person for the job. Tom later told me that he felt like some invisible force was behind the last-minute switch, nudging everything in the right direction. You gotta love those helping hands!

⌣

Mary giggled uncontrollably over the phone. "It's a miracle, Ann. It's one of those personal oracles you're always talking about."

She proceeded to share the highlight of her day. "It was my responsibility to get the copy for the fund-raiser to the newspaper, and today was the deadline. I've written dozens of these news releases, but this one was a struggle. It felt like something important was missing. I knew that if I could talk to Dawn, she would polish it up in a second. Unfortunately she was traveling in California, and I didn't have her new cell number. It looked like I was going to have to settle for the way it was. Then my phone rang. When I heard her voice on the other end, I screamed." Not quite the response Dawn expected.

Talk about perfect timing. At the moment Mary's frustration peaked, Dawn happened to call her. Dawn was riding the train from Burbank to San Diego and wanted to see if her new phone worked. Mary explained what was going on, and within five minutes the two of them had wordsmithed the article into perfect form.

As we go about the business of living, we never know what role we might play in a synchronistic scenario. Ah, the wonder of personal oracles.

SIGNS AND SYMBOLS

Signs and symbols are like billboards announcing messages designed for your eyes only. Some contain messages that are as clearly understood as stop-and-go traffic lights. Other signs and symbols operate more like secret codes that require a bit of deciphering. If you take the time to reflect on what's happening in your life and how the sign or symbol relates to your specific circumstances, have faith—the message will emerge.

Take this incident of the fortune cookie in the shopping cart that my friend Sarah shared with me. It was Monday, the beginning of the week, and already Sarah felt harried. Lately she'd been finding herself forced to deal with important details that consumed more of her time than usual. Her first meeting of the day was a forty-five-minute drive from her studio. She glanced at the clock. She would just make it. She had driven less than a few miles when she felt her blood sugar drop, a symptom of her hypoglycemia. She had forgotten her protein bars. She knew she needed to eat some protein or face the consequences of a mushy mind and no energy. Irritated and with her stress level on the rise, she pulled into a market.

She was just about to plop her purse onto the seat of the shopping cart when she noticed the strangest of objects. Perched on the seat was one perfect little unwrapped fortune cookie. A tempting piece of paper peeked out of one end. Sara couldn't resist. She broke open the cookie and pulled out the fortune. "Your patience will be rewarded."

Sarah took the message to heart. She made a point to relax. She arrived late to the meeting, but her mind wasn't mushy and her energy was intact. Sharing the story of the fortune cookie with her client saved the day. In fact, she says it was one of her most productive meetings ever.

The message also resonated with Sarah on a deeper level. At the time she found the message, she was unhappy in her job and had been contemplating sending out résumés. But her intuition nagged at her to wait. As she said, "The cookie message was a big confirmation that things would work out. It had the impact of the clouds parting and a voice from above booming down on me."

⌣

Have you ever wondered if you were on the right path? Personal oracles, like the one Sarah received, often appear to confirm if we are cruising along in the right direction or to direct us to change our vector. While writing one day, I began to question if I was heading in the right direction. As I began to second-guess myself, I felt a nudge to take a break, so I made a cup of hot tea and walked outside. That's when I spotted this amazing image in a cloud.

There was no doubt about it. The universe was giving me a sign: a big thumbs-up.

I set my tea down, ran inside, and grabbed my camera. When I returned to my office I felt confident that I was on the right path. It was a clear sign. The universe was supporting me all the way.

When I photographed the thumbs-up I didn't notice the little smiling eyes and face to the right of the hand. Nor did I see what looks like a wrist and arm connected to the fist. Or the neck that's under the chin. I still get a kick out of the mouth—it looks to me like it's serious about confirming the thumbs-up. Photographing an image can sometimes provide information that we don't notice at the time the personal oracle is being delivered. In this case, that couldn't have been truer.

⌣

Julie was a weaver with a dream; she wanted to teach fiber art. Her daughter Ashley also had a dream—to design and sell a line of edgy clothing. The mother and daughter worked together in a local weaver's studio that displayed some of Julie's wall hangings and blankets replicating ancient designs. Working in this environment every day enabled mother and daughter to envision how their dreams could combine into one business. They discussed

how they could sell their products and even teach others to weave, spin wool into yarn, work with natural dyes, and create fiber art.

For a few years it was only talk, until one day at the studio Julie spotted something lying on the windowsill. At first glance it looked like a delicate filigree pendant inset with tiny jewels. She looked closer and discovered that the iridescent green and blue figure was a dragonfly with its wings outstretched. It was as perfect as if someone had mounted it in a frame. Ashley lined the bottom of a box with soft, smooth fabric and placed the dragonfly gently inside, like a treasure. They agreed—this was no random dragonfly. It was a sign that mirrored a message for them. But what was the message?

They researched the symbolic significance of the dragonfly and discovered it was a damselfly—the slender, delicate version of a dragonfly. They read: "If a dragonfly has shown up, look for change to occur. Are you resisting change when you shouldn't?" It was their call to action, and they knew it.

They rented a small studio and began teaching classes in the evenings and on weekends. They ran ads in local magazines, appeared on radio talk shows, and networked over the Internet. Within a year they moved to a larger space and expanded their fiber arts business to include weavings and Ashley's edgy line of clothing. Thanks to the dragonfly that mirrored a challenge, they transformed their dreams into reality.

INVISIBLE MOVING SIDEWALKS

An invisible moving sidewalk is composed of a series of synchronistic events that are designed to carry you to a specific destination. Think people movers in large airports. Except these sidewalks can be life-altering. They refocus us in a positive direction. Invisible moving sidewalks transport people to new opportunities—new locations, new jobs, new relationships, new health, new insights—and even bring us to the right place at the right time to lend a helping hand. We usually can't tell when we step onto one, but when we arrive at the destination and look back, we say, "Oh, I get it, that's what was going on!" It's like being given a sneak preview into how the universe sets everything in place to respond to a need.

Noreen stepped onto an invisible moving sidewalk when she and her husband had a knock-down, drag-out argument. She stormed out of the house, slamming the door behind her. "Get a life!" she yelled.

She drove around for a while to cool off and ended up at the library. Inside, she spotted a bulletin board with a flyer advertising an annual writing conference. She ran her finger down the list of seminars and presenters and noticed the names of some of her favorite authors, along with unfamiliar experts from the publishing world. For a small fee, attendees could even make an appointment with one of the experts to critique their writing. "Wish I was still writing," Noreen said. Embarrassed by the unexpected sound of her voice in the hush of the library, she glanced around to see if anyone had heard. Noreen stood there toying with the idea of attending but her little internal voice kept whispering, "*You're not qualified.*"

The next day at the water cooler, Noreen overheard a coworker talking excitedly about the Wrangling with Writing conference she was attending that weekend. When Noreen expressed an interest in attending, her friend suggested they go together.

Noreen brought a blank notebook and pens to the conference, made copious notes during the sessions, and by the end of the two days she was awash with new ideas. Her passion for writing had been rekindled. Before leaving the conference, she asked for the date of next year's conference and added it to her pocket calendar. Now she had incentive and a time frame. Noreen knew in her heart that she would have something worth sharing next year, something for one of those experts to critique.

Noreen stepped onto the sidewalk when she argued with her husband. Choosing the library as a refuge, seeing the flyer on the bulletin board, and running into her coworker as the woman was talking about the conference were synchronistic events that led her toward her final destination of becoming a writer.

⟶

A woman in Kansas writes:

I don't usually travel with my husband when he delivers bowling equipment to his clients, but this was going to be a long work weekend for him that entailed a lot of overnight driving from one state to another. We loaded the bowling equipment and supplies into the car and set out. We were just about to turn onto the highway when Keith realized some key equipment was missing. Around we turned and headed back to the bowling alley to pick up the missing balls. "Wait," I said. "Didn't you take those balls to Spring-field last week?" The look on his face said it all. It was already later than we'd planned to leave and adding extra miles to get over to Springfield was not what we wanted. Keith called and verified that the equipment was still there, and we altered our route and mentally extended our trip another five hours.

It was about one in the morning by the time we arrived at the bowling alley in Springfield, Missouri. Keith's friend met us and helped us get loaded and back on the road as quickly as possible. A half an hour later we were driving in the middle of nowhere, between Springfield and Kansas City, when we came across a banged-up truck sitting in the middle of the highway at an angle and a woman wander-ing along the shoulder of the road. We pulled over. The woman had hit a deer and was clearly shaken and upset. We were loaded down with bowling equipment so the options were limited. She used our cell phone to call a

friend, and then we waited with her until they arrived to
pick her up.

Keith and I look back now and marvel at how we
wouldn't have been anywhere near that area if he hadn't
left the bowling balls in Springfield, an oversight that forced
us to detour in that direction. He also said that he would
have felt uncomfortable stopping and waiting with a
stranded female out in the middle of nowhere. He wasn't
alone, though. Because the trip involved extensive driving,
he had needed a second driver—me.

This invisible moving sidewalk twisted and turned and eventually delivered these Good Samaritans to the right place at the right time.

Here's a more complex invisible moving sidewalk, with twists and turns and threads of significant interconnections running all over the place.

Paul was headed home when he realized that he'd left his cell phone on his desk. The turmoil in his personal life that had plagued him throughout the summer had clearly thrown him off balance. He was doing his best not to give in to feelings of being overwhelmed by his fledgling business. Not to mention the latest drama involving his ex, the mother of his teenage son. He made a U-turn and headed back to his warehouse. The sun caught his eyes and he popped down the visor. Halfway through a busy intersection, something crashed against the side of his truck. He bolted out of the pickup. A man lay sprawled on his back. Twenty feet away was a twisted motorcycle. Paul knelt on the pavement and grasped the man's hand and squeezed it while trying to determine if he was conscious. He felt a weak squeeze back. Thank God the man was conscious.

Paul leaned over the injured stranger. "You're going to be all right. I won't let anything happen to you," he said.

Paul pulled his T-shirt off and placed it under the man's head to make him more comfortable. No helmet was in sight. Paul held the man's hand again. His stomach jumped into his throat. He couldn't believe what he'd done to this fellow. He had always taken such pride in being the person who took care of everyone. Now here he was, a villain.

At the police station waiting to be interrogated, Paul felt shattered. He called his best friend for moral support. "I do understand that you hit the motorcyclist, but this doesn't feel like your accident," she said. "It feels like you're playing your part in a larger scenario." Though he still felt awful for causing the accident, Paul listened.

"Thanks for being there for me," he said, and hung up. A sergeant walked over to Paul and rested his hand on his shoulder. "Come with me," he said. He'd been at the scene and witnessed Paul's unusual connection with the injured man. The officer brought him over to his desk and they sat down. "I saw that you didn't want to let go of his hand when they put him in the ambulance. I'm not supposed to do this, but here." He slid a report in front of Paul. The motorcyclist was listed in serious condition with some broken ribs and a head injury, but was expected to make a full recovery. Though somewhat relieved, Paul still felt sick inside.

He decided to run his friend's theory by the sergeant about how he might be playing a part in a larger scenario. The sergeant reflected for a moment. "Sure, there's always another layer of stuff going on." Then the officer leaned back in his chair, clasped his hands behind his head, and shared his own personal experiences. Numerous times he could have been shot, but was saved by a series of inexplicable circumstances that were beyond his control. Paul knew he couldn't shrug off responsibility for the accident, yet looking at it from a larger perspective made him think about his own life. If he hadn't been feeling overwhelmed, he would have been more alert driving. Maybe it was time to begin resolving his personal issues.

Days later the injured man's girlfriend called Paul. "We've decided not to follow the insurance company's advice. We're not going to sue." She went on to say how her boyfriend was deeply touched by the way Paul had rushed to his side and then stayed with him until the EMTs actually pulled them apart. Paul and the girlfriend didn't have a long conversation, but it was long enough for him to learn that her boyfriend was estranged from his family and that the concern and supportive energy he had received from Paul had been a much needed blessing.

After a few court appearances, Paul was sentenced to thirty-seven hours of community service for running a red light. Paul had always been quick to lend a helping hand, so the idea of serving the community made him feel better. He also promised himself that he would do what it took to work through his problems.

By the time he returned to court to hand in his record of community service, he had sought the professional counseling and advice that helped him make needed changes in his personal life. His business was also heading in a better direction. He faced the same judge who had officiated over all of his court appearances. When the short proceeding ended, Paul asked to approach the bench. In a confidential voice, he asked the judge for his take on the idea of Paul being part of the larger purpose of the man's motorcycle accident. The judge, who'd always been a bit remote and judgelike, listened to the premise, then turned his head to one side for a few seconds. When he turned back, his face had softened and his persona changed. "There is always a larger picture. I watch it play out every day."

Paul walked the two blocks to the parking lot, his spirits lighter than they had been in a long time. Only one cloud dotted the bright blue sky above him. He replayed the events of the past four months. A sense of gratefulness flooded through him. Before he climbed into the truck, he looked up at the sky. The cloud had disappeared. Now, only a blue sky filled with yellow sunshine hung over his life.

Paul was pitched unwittingly onto an invisible moving sidewalk that challenged him to take responsibility for his actions. Yes, he had caused what could have been a very serious accident. But beyond that accident was a larger picture, a perspective that Paul's friend, the sergeant, and the judge helped validate. Paul needed to address significant issues affecting him. When he finally stepped off the invisible moving sidewalk, he was rewarded with a personal oracle—a cloud that disappeared—confirming that order was returning to his life.

SPONTANEOUS VS. REQUESTED ORACLES

All personal oracles respond to a need. As you become more acquainted with personal oracles, however, you will notice that some oracles are spontaneous while others are requested. Spontaneous personal oracles arrive on the scene before we even know we need their assistance. These include the voice Alan heard, Rhonda's hummingbird warning, and the license plate with GVT that slowed the driver down before she saw the speed camera.

A requested oracle comes in response to spoken words or silent thoughts or prayers. The request can be clearly and consciously made, as in the case of my road trip from Taos when I asked for protection and was shown an unchanging heart-shaped cloud. Requests also occur at a subconscious level. Noreen's frustrated scream of "get a life" resulted in her being directed to a writers' conference and a brand-new writing life. Similarly, Sara was fed up with what she calls "fiddly things" that kept derailing her plans, and she wished that they would go away. The personal oracle didn't make the fiddly things that were plaguing her disappear, but it provided a clue that helped her get back on track.

PERSONAL ORACLE FORMULA

Whether a personal oracle is a mirror, a conduit, synchronicity, a sign, a symbol, or an invisible moving sidewalk, and whether it is spontaneous or requested, it always consists of three parts.

1. A need or request
2. A delivery system
3. A message

NEED + DELIVERY SYSTEM + MESSAGE = PERSONAL ORACLE

This formula serves as another tool to help you identify and confirm your personal oracles. You can see how the formula works by applying it to Rhonda's hummingbird oracle. In Rhonda's case, the need was to protect Rhonda and her little dogs from the pack of wild dogs rampaging in the area. A need or request functions like a summons to the universe; it's a call to action. In this case, the call was urgent.

Imagine the call going out across the web of interconnections to any available and willing delivery system within range of Rhonda. In this case the urgent call was received and accepted by a tiny hummingbird. It became the delivery system. This hummingbird "knew" to fly directly in front of Rhonda's face and then hover in midair to stop Rhonda and her dogs from continuing their walk. The word "danger" that kept flashing in Rhonda's mind was a telepathic message that left her with no doubt about what to do. The message's urgency was heightened by the sensations of fear that coursed through her body.

Remember that the delivery system that transports a message is always tailor-made to resonate specifically with you and your circumstances. Many of us might have brushed away a hummingbird hovering directly in front of our face, or ducked or dodged out of the way. Some might have ignored the telepathic message. Rhonda, however, chose to pay attention to what was happening and trust her senses and intuition.

With time and practice, you will begin to recognize your personal oracles. They may be as dramatic as Rhonda's or as quiet and unassuming as Sara's fortune cookie. You may experience more than one in a day, or days may pass without the occurrence of one personal oracle. Regardless, when you do receive and recognize your personal oracles, be prepared to experience a deeper sense of joy, comfort, gratefulness, and even awe at the connections within our universe and the guidance those connections offer. They are nothing less than amazing.

As you will read, many of the saints and celebrities in the next chapter have experienced the influence and wisdom of personal oracles. Some of these experiences have even changed the course of history. Have fun exploring their stories.

Chapter 3

Everyone Has Personal Oracles

*And above all, watch with glittering eyes the
world around you because the greatest secrets are
always hidden in the most unlikely places. Those
who don't believe in magic will never find it.*

—ROALD DAHL

If it's Oscar night you will find me settled in front of the TV. So
I was "there" in 2006 when one of my favorite actors took the
stage to accept the Oscar for Best Actor. He had won for his
powerful portrayal of the Ugandan dictator Idi Amin in *The Last
King of Scotland*. Forest Whitaker stood at the podium, appearing calm and grounded. He remained silent, as if letting this
extraordinary moment settle into the very heart of his being.
Finally he spoke. "I could feel the breath on my neck and the tingling on my body. For me it is like my ancestors speaking to me."
It truly was an inspiring moment.

And unexpected. A personal oracle noted and even announced at an Academy Awards ceremony. Who would have
thought?

Well, it made me curious. Personal oracles, after all, aren't just phenomena of the present. They are as old as time and have been embraced by people in all walks of life. Wouldn't it be interesting to know how personal oracles have affected the lives of famous people we admire? Following are personal oracle stories that involve individuals many of us have heard of or read about in this century and previous centuries. Even if you don't recognize some of these historical figures and/or celebrities, their stories will inspire you to keep your eyes open and your senses alert.

⌐

Ancient history tells us that in the fourth century B.C., Alexander the Great consulted with astrologers, oracles, and soothsayers on a regular basis. One account suggests that he received but failed to heed an important prophetic message. Alexander was on a journey to Babylon when he felt impelled to consult his personal wise men about his future.

"Do not enter that town," they replied. "It is evilly fatal to thee. Be warned in time, for the stars are ever true. As their light scintillates and makes our nights a marvel of truth and glory, so the truth of their language shall eternally shine to him who knows how to read them. Flee from this town where thy fatal star reigns." Alexander was deeply impressed by this warning and did avoid the city of Babylon, but only for a while. Eventually he would meet his death in that city.

Acting on a gut feeling to seek guidance is one thing. Following that guidance can be an entirely different matter.

⌐

Who would have thought that one tiny spider going about its business back in the 1300s could serve as a personal oracle that would encourage countless people to try, try again? The story has it that Robert the Bruce, who became one of Scotland's most revered kings, was hiding out in a cave in a desperate attempt to avoid being captured by his English pursuers. While biding his time, he became fascinated by the slow, deliberate process of a spider diligently weaving its web. The spider would weave and fall, weave and fall, weave and fall. Its tenacity inspired Robert the Bruce, mirroring the encouragement he needed just when he needed it the most. Some even say that this hero originated the saying "If at first you don't succeed, try, try again." After numerous attempts, Robert the Bruce eventually led Scotland to independence from England. Robert the Bruce and his spider remind us that the guidance we need can appear in even the most mundane form.

⌐

The following story is a perfect example of how a personal oracle can change the course of a life and continue to encourage people for more than half a millennium. English children and adults alike are familiar with the legend of the Bow Bells and the man behind it, Lord Mayor Richard Whittington. Many know his story from a famous scene in the pantomime of Dick Whittington and his cat that is still performed throughout England. In the pantomime, Dick, a boy from a poor family in Gloucester, walks to London to make his fortune, accompanied by his cat. In the city he meets with little success. Feeling discouraged, Dick and his cat are heading home by way of Highgate Hill when he hears the bells of Saint Mary-le-Bow Church ring out three times. Dick believes the bells are sending him a message to turn back.

He turns back, and later makes his fortune; strangely enough, he is elected Lord Mayor of London three times. Even those who question the existence of his pet cat seem to embrace the timely message the young Richard Whittington received from the Bow Bells. Today his statue stands outside the Whittington Hospital on Highgate Hill as a tribute to the boy who heeded the guidance of the Bow Bells.

⌣

Some famous examples of personal oracle guidance are right in front of us. Take Sir Isaac Newton. We associate Newton with the apple that fell on his head and led him to discover gravity. But the question is: Could this apple have been acting as a personal oracle? From what we know of Newton, he might have said yes. Though he is most commonly known for his breakthrough theory of gravity, history suggests that all of his work was influenced by his experiences with the mystical. Born in the 1600s, when astronomy and astrology were considered to be one and the same, this highly respected alchemist looked to the heavens to assist him in his quest to decode the mysteries of the universe. Newton's knowledge of the paranormal is as well documented as his knowledge of the measurable. It has been suggested that Newton was not the first of the Age of Reason but the last of the magicians.

⌣

Was Mahatma Gandhi a saint?

It's reported that people called him a saint trying to be a politician. Gandhi said he was a politician trying to be a saint.

While every move Gandhi made toward nonviolence seemed to be spontaneous, his actions were prompted by a deep intuition that often came to him in the eleventh hour.

This was never more evident than in 1930, when Great Britain imposed a salt tax on India that forbade the processing of salt. It was an attempt to tighten governmental control over India and make the country dependent on the British for salt, a necessary commodity in any tropical country.

At the stroke of midnight on January 1, the Indian Congress Party took a stand. They raised the flag of a new nation and ushered in the struggle for complete independence from Great Britain. Everyone looked to Gandhi to see what would happen next. Weeks passed as the threat of violence mounted. Gandhi remained silent. The British government waited anxiously, afraid to arrest him and afraid to leave him free.

At long last, after waiting for his eleventh-hour inspiration, Gandhi found the solution in a dream. The answer was simple. He proposed marching 240 miles with seventy-eight of his most trusted ashram followers to the little coastal town of Dandi. There, salt from the sea lay on the sand, free for the taking.

The stage was set for India to be turned upside down. Gandhi's march swelled to several thousand followers by the time they reached the sea. After prayers were offered, Gandhi spoke to the large crowd. Then, purposefully, he picked up a tiny lump of salt. Within moments everyone followed Gandhi's passive defiance and picked up salt everywhere along the coast.

A month later, Gandhi was arrested and thrown into a prison full of his fellow protesters. The Salt March started a series of protests that closed many British shops and mills. Horrible violence followed. When Gandhi's nonviolent followers did not defend themselves against the clubs of policemen, many died instantly.

Gandhi's personal oracle played a part in what eventually became India's successful quest for independence.

⌐

If you were around in the 1960s, you probably remember the Beatles' high-profile journey to India in search of Truth. On the other hand, John Lennon's extraordinary search for guidance in the last years of his life went pretty much unnoticed.

Having lost confidence in his writing and recording, Lennon consulted an African oracle. The seer advised him that in order to become psychically aligned, he would need to journey southeast across the ocean, which meant traveling through the Bermuda Triangle. She warned him that the trip would involve extreme danger.

Out on the ocean, John felt like he was fulfilling a part of his destiny that he had avoided for too long. Both his Irish father and grandfather had been men of the sea, and John had always felt a longing to fulfill that Lennon itch to travel the high seas. Lennon described experiencing an "overwhelming sensation of freedom." Then the ship entered the Bermuda Triangle.

Twenty-foot swells and gale-force winds whipped the boat for two days, rocking it like a never-ending roller-coaster ride. One after another of the crew became seasick. John felt certain he was facing an untimely death at sea. When the captain became incapacitated, he ordered Lennon to take the wheel and hold the threatened ship steady. John stood on the deck lashed to the rails of the wheelhouse like Ahab strapped to the whale, petrified by the force driving the ship into the waves. Spray stung his face and streamed over his glasses. As his watch wore on, John felt his courage rising. "It was just like going onstage," he recollected. "At first you panic, and then you're ready to throw up your guts. But once you get out there, you start doing your stuff. You forget your fears and you get high on your performance. . . . Once I accepted the reality of the situation, I lost my fear and began to enjoy the experience."

As the sea rose before him, he shouted back to it in defiance, singing chanteys, sailor songs, and old ballads he had heard growing up in Liverpool. The experience proved life-changing. This voyage not only restored John's confidence in himself, but rebooted his creativity and inspired him to write and record what would turn out to be his final album, *Double Fantasy*. Like most of us at one time or another, John Lennon needed help getting back on track. Knowing where to look for guidance and then following it is the key.

You might assume that a central figure in the magical realism movement in Latin American literature would have the edge on being tuned in to the mysteries of everyday life. But even novelist and Nobel Prize winner Gabriel García Márquez missed this one.

García Márquez tells of the time he answered his doorbell to find a stranger delivering a prophetic personal oracle. The stranger said, "You must change the electric iron's cord—it's faulty!" Then, thinking he had come to the wrong house, the stranger promptly apologized and left. Half an hour later, García Márquez's iron burst into flames, as a result of a faulty cord. This mystifying message that foreshadowed a later event is encouragement to venture outside the restrictions of our three-dimensional paradigm.

Wayne Dyer describes this personal oracle as the most profound mystical experience in his sixty-five years. It occurred on the day Dyer completed the second to last chapter of his book *Inspiration*. He read it over the phone to his editor and then went for his daily hourlong walk along the beach near his home in Hawaii. For some reason, however, he decided to take a slightly different route along a grassy area that runs adjacent to the beach. He thought about his friend Jack Boland, a Unity minister in Detroit who had crossed over about ten years earlier. Jack had loved monarch butterflies and often told stories of these paper-thin creatures that migrated thousands of miles in high winds and returned to the same branch on the same tree where they first emerged from cocoons. Before Jack passed, Dyer had presented him with a special paperweight containing a perfectly preserved monarch.

He was walking along feeling relieved and grateful that he had completed the chapter when a monarch butterfly landed on the ground three feet in front of him. The butterfly remained in place as he continued walking toward it, then finally flapped its wings a couple of times and flew away. Puzzled, Dyer watched the little creature. It flew about forty or fifty yards and then, to his amazement, made a U-turn and flew right back, only this time it landed directly on Dyer's finger. What followed borders on the incredible.

For the next two and a half hours the butterfly became his constant companion, sitting first on one hand, then moving to the other hand. This little guy had no intention of flying away. Instead he seemed to be trying to communicate by moving his wings back and forth and even opening and closing his tiny mouth, as if attempting to speak. Dyer sat on the ground with his new friend for a half hour or so, then decided to try to get a photo. He walked the mile home, this time along the beach. The strong winds buffeted the butterfly's wings, but it held fast to Dyer's finger and at one point even moved from one hand to the other, making no attempt to leave.

Back at home, Dyer left his butterfly friend, whom he was now calling "Jack," sitting on the newly completed handwritten chapter, "The Language of Spirit." He returned to his desk and the waiting butterfly with a camera. He put his hand next to Jack and watched him jump right back onto his finger. They posed for a photograph.

Dyer spent the next hour communing with this butterfly and pondering what he calls "the most unprecedented and out-of-the-ordinary spiritual episode I've ever encountered." Then he set Jack back on the manuscript and went to take a long, hot shower. When Dyer returned, he placed his finger near the butterfly as he had done so often in the last few hours, but now it seemed a totally different creature. The butterfly fluttered away, landed on the table, flapped its wings twice, and flew off.

Dyer had felt the energy of his friend Jack in the butterfly. Anyone witnessing the interplay between the man and butterfly probably would not have picked up on this connection. But that's what personal oracles are all about—being special to the one receiving the guidance, comfort, reassurance, or whatever message is being delivered.

⌒

Early in his career, journalist and network news correspondent Byron Pitts trudged down the sidewalk in the heat of a Georgia summer, discouraged and tired of worrying about how to pay his bills on the limited salary of a local broadcaster. The long hours and constant pressures had not propelled Pitts where he had dreamed of going. He was questioning whether broadcasting was the right path after all when he stepped into the intersection. Suddenly, he sensed something to his right and jumped back onto the curb. A car zipped past, just inches away. In its wake flew a couple of birds that circled in front of Pitts, who realized he had narrowly escaped death. The words to his mother's favorite hymn popped into his mind. "His eye is on the sparrow, and I know He watches me."

In that moment Pitts felt like a little boy sitting next to his mama in the pew at New Shiloh, praying that someday he'd be able to overcome his stutter. That did happen. Spirit had watched over and helped him. The bird messengers reminded him that he was still being protected and guided. He realized he had been focused on his doubts, replaying a tape of himself at his worst. He hit the off button and reconnected to the reasons he wanted to be a broadcast journalist—telling stories that help others, informing and inspiring people. Pitts continued along the path of broadcasting. The hard work paid off. CBS offered him a position on *60 Minutes*, a dream come true.

The birds that darted up and circled in front of him had held up a mirror of memories, and those memories offered the inspiration he needed to continue pursuing his dream.

⌒

There seems to be no limit to the talents of this twenty-first-century American singer, actress, director, and songwriter. Barbra Streisand is one of the most commercially and critically successful entertainers in modern entertainment history.

What you may not know is that the encouragement for Streisand's 1983 movie *Yentl* came from her father. But not while he was alive. Four years before the film was released, she attended a séance where she received two messages from her dad. The first message, *"Sorry,"* astonished her. Few people knew that she was angry with him for leaving her. He died when she was fifteen months old. The second message was *"Sing proud."* Barbra said, "I know it sounds crazy, but I knew it was my father telling me to have the courage of my convictions, so I made *Yentl*, and I did sing proud." Barbra not only sang in the starring role, but also made her debut as a director, becoming the first woman to produce, direct, star in, and cowrite a screenplay for a feature film. The film received five Oscar nominations, winning for Best Original Song Score, and five Golden Globe nominations, winning for Best Director.

⌒

Best known for his iconic TV portrayal in the seventies of the lollipop-licking detective Kojak, the late, great Greek-born actor Telly Savalas reported this amazing incident in multiple televised interviews. Records of the accounts vary, but the core of the experience remains the same.

Savalas received a personal oracle delivered by what he called a "ghost." It occurred in the wee hours of a summer morning in 1954. He was driving home from a friend's house on Long Island to his home in New York around three A.M. when he ran out of gas. He decided to walk to a nearby freeway where he knew a filling station would still be open for service.

As he set off on the daunting walk, he heard a voice call out, *"I'll give you a lift."*

Savalas looked around and saw a man dressed in a white suit standing beside a big black Cadillac. He admitted to being a bit shaken since he hadn't heard the car pull up beside him or the car door open. The man didn't look dangerous, so he accepted a ride from this Good Samaritan.

At the filling station Savalas was embarrassed to discover that he didn't have enough money to pay for the gas. The Good Samaritan didn't seem to mind and said Savalas could pay him back later. They drove back to the car and filled the tank. The man wrote his name and phone number on a scrap of paper and Savalas thanked him for all he had done.

The next day Savalas dialed the number on the piece of paper. When a woman answered, he recounted how her husband had helped him the night before. The woman said that was impossible. Her husband had died three years earlier. Shocked but intrigued, the celebrity described the big black Cadillac. The stunned woman said it was the same as her husband's car. She began to cry when he described the clothes the man was wearing; they were the clothes her husband had been buried in. Savalas eventually met the widow and showed her the piece of paper on which the man had written his number. She was sure it was her husband's handwriting.

Receiving personal oracles from loved ones who have passed on, as Forest Whitaker and Barbra Streisand did, might seem unusual yet somewhat logical. Family helps family. But when help manifests at the perfect time in the form of a stranger who has already passed on, you know the universe's helping hand is indeed extensive. As Savalas's character Kojak would say, "Who loves ya, baby?!"

ANN BOLINGER-McQUADE

Before hosting the popular PBS series *Mystery* from 1981 to 1989, acclaimed actor Vincent Price experienced a mysterious personal oracle that foreshadowed the death of a close friend. He was traveling by plane from Hollywood to New York on November 15, 1958, when he happened to look up from the book he was reading. There, in brilliant lettering across the sky, he saw the sentence "TYRONE POWER IS DEAD." After only a few seconds the words disappeared. The phrase shocked him. Nobody sitting near him seemed to have noticed, so he decided not to mention the incident to anyone. He even began to doubt that he had seen the words. When the plane landed, however, Vincent learned the truth. Actor Tyrone Power, his dear friend, had died suddenly a few hours earlier.

English singer-songwriter Amy Winehouse was best known for her powerful contralto voice and eclectic mix of musical genres. In 2006 this multitalented performer, who is often credited with revitalizing the British music scene, won five Grammy Awards, including one for Best New Artist. By 2007, Winehouse's problems with substance abuse and her self-destructive behavior became regular tabloid news. In 2008, she faced a series of health complications that threatened both her career and her life. In the summer of 2009, Winehouse may have gotten more than she expected. During one of her regular sessions with a clairvoyant, she heard Michael Jackson's distinctive voice. Michael was instructing her to clean up her act. The King of Pop delivered this urgent personal oracle a few days after his untimely death. One wonders if Michael was trying to save Amy's life since it was too late to save his own.

⟜

During her lifetime, Lucille Ball was one of the most popular and influential stars in America. Her career launched in the 1930s and continued well into the seventies. Reruns of *I Love Lucy* still fill television screens with the antics of this spirited redhead. The beloved show might never have starred Lucille Ball without this timely thumbs-up personal oracle.

In 1951, Ball was considering a proposal for what was to become the *I Love Lucy* series. She waffled about accepting the role until she had a dream. In the dream, her close friend Carole Lombard suggested that she "give it a whirl." The renowned actress had died nine years earlier in a plane crash. Ball accepted the role, and the rest is TV Land history.

From saints to celebrities, we all receive personal oracle messages straight from the divine mystery. As you probably noticed in the above examples, each message is tailor-made to meet an individual's needs. Whether or not we choose to heed those messages is a personal choice. Before you face that decision, you need to recognize how personal oracles speak to you.

PART II

Investigating
Your World of
Personal Oracles

Chapter 4

What Speaks to You?
Clouds, Cledons, and Everything in Between

One day Chuang-tzu and a friend were walking
along a riverbank. When he exclaimed,
  "How delightfully the fishes are enjoying
  themselves in the water!"
  "You are not a fish," his friend said. "How do
  you know whether or not the fishes are enjoy-
  ing themselves?"
  "You are not me," Chuang-tzu said. "How do you
  know that I do not know that the fishes are
  enjoying themselves?"

—Zen Buddhist teaching

Personal oracles are just that: personal. They resonate with
you and you alone according to your unique needs. What
may be a personal oracle to you may be just another cloud or
bird or butterfly to someone else. Remember my friend Georgia,

who encountered a symmetrical tree on her walk? Let's say that you and Georgia had been walking together and came upon that tree. You might have said something like, "What a gorgeous tree," and snapped a photo of it. Or maybe you wouldn't have said anything at all, just thought to yourself how unusual its shape was. Georgia, on the other hand, stopped and studied the tree. The perfect symmetry of its limbs spoke to her, nudged her to examine her own life and identify what was missing from it. It helped her realize that her life needed balance. For Georgia, the tree was a personal oracle. For you, it was a work of nature, beautiful and elegant, but for whatever reason, it did not serve as a personal oracle for you.

What this means, of course, is that no one besides you can identify your personal oracles. Learning to work with oracles is as solo an activity as reading a book or listening to music through headphones. It's a very personal experience. Of course, it's fun to share your personal oracles with others, just like it's fun to share with others literature and music that excites you. But in order to share, you have to locate and identify that book, that song, that personal oracle.

I've compiled some guidelines to help you know where to begin looking for your personal oracles, along with some fascinating stories of how others have experienced theirs. Think of these as jumping-off points for your journey into those hidden dimensions where your messages are hiding in plain sight. You will notice that some oracles fit into more than one category. Once again, there is no right or wrong way to categorize personal oracles. In fact, after you get the gist of how oracles work, the need to categorize them will fall by the wayside.

- Clouds
- Resonance through the senses
- Animals
- Earth whispers
- Songs, books, and the written word
- Universal symbols and numerology
- Memory imprints and seeds of our ancestors
- Cledons

CLOUDS

I've yet to meet a person who hasn't gazed at clouds with wonder
and delight, even if they never considered that clouds could serve
as personal oracles. As you know, for me clouds deliver messages
of all kinds. Check out this everyday cloud that spoke to me during a frantic day. This striking image mirrored what I was doing:
running around like my hair was on fire. When I figured out its
message, I laughed and relaxed. A sense of calm settled over me,
which I'm sure benefited my overall well-being.

Clouds also have delivered gentle messages of comfort and support just when I needed them most, like the day I was headed out to the vet clinic to visit our beloved golden retriever Rusty Bear. He was being treated for lymphoma. A gut feeling told me to take my camera in case I spotted any special clouds. So I did. I was still upstairs when I walked past an open deck door and an energetic tug drew my attention outside to this heartwarming cloud formation in the sky.

The cloud image on the left is the cloud as it appeared. The outline on the right is what I saw: a peaceful Rusty Bear cradled within an abundance of heart-shaped clouds. Although I didn't sense that these symbols of love predicted his recovery, I did feel they were telling me that love and protection surrounded him and were keeping him comfortable during this traumatic time.

Has a cloud ever changed your mood or inspired you in some way? I have lots of friends who stay on the alert for cloud messages. One Valentine's Day, a friend noticed the shape of a long-stemmed rose, and felt like it was a gift, a sign of love from her deceased lover. Another friend noticed a smiling teddy bear, heart bib and all, that looked exactly like the mascot for the band the Grateful Dead. She had no doubt that her friend who had passed on was sending her a message to remind her of him and all those concerts they had attended together. Early one morning a coworker of mine opened the screen door to let her dogs out and out of habit glanced at the sky. To her surprise, she saw two huge eyes with distinct pupils looking back at her. She immediately recognized the familiar energy of divine presence. This friend felt like the eyes of God were gazing into her soul, validating everything she was doing to make a big change in her life.

I'm not suggesting that you go around with your head in the clouds, but do check them out. You never know what wonders await you.

RESONANCE THROUGH THE SENSES

When you're on the lookout for personal oracles, pay attention to your senses. In addition to the obvious sense of sight, messages may resonate through hearing, touch, and smell. (I have yet to experience or hear of a personal oracle coming through the sense of taste, but hey, in the world of personal oracles, never rule out any possibility!)

Mary was exhausted. She had been in labor for twelve hours and now the doctor was instructing her to push. She felt the edges of panic. Where was she supposed to get the energy to do that?

"Pace yourself. You can do it," whispered a voice in her ear.

Mary recognized her father's voice. But he had died ten years earlier.

"Stay calm, and pace yourself. You'll be fine."

Mary knew she wasn't imagining hearing her father's encouragement. She knew he was in the room supporting her. She followed his advice and centered her concentration and breath on each push. She replayed the words "you can do it" over and over, like a mantra encouraging her forward. Twenty minutes later, Mary gave birth to her first child, a beautiful, healthy little girl. Mary says she has a feeling her dad stayed with her to welcome his new grandchild into the world. "And if it's possible, I know he kissed her on the top of her tiny head."

⌐

When she was twelve, Ellen and her family drove from Chicago to Orlando, Florida, during spring break. She and her parents and younger brother left the cold and snow early on a Saturday morning and arrived in Nashville just before dinnertime. The sixty-degree weather and magnolia-scented air felt enticing, so, after dinner at a restaurant, the family ambled through the grounds of the pretty state capitol.

> *I remember the area around the main building had different levels of plazas and walkways. We had just ascended some stairs that delivered us to the edge of an expansive plaza. To me it looked like it was made out of white marble, smooth and open. I loved being out of the cold, being out of school, being on vacation. I felt so free. I had an inclination to run across the open space to the other end. There*

wasn't a railing, and I assumed that I could jump down to the next landing. I started to run, but then the oddest thing happened.

I felt a pair of arms grab me around the middle. It was like someone was standing behind me and put their arms around me to hold me back. For a moment, I wanted to ignore the feeling. I wanted to run. I loved running. But something inside me said to pay attention and obey.

We walked across the plaza and when we got to the edge, I peered over. It was a ten-foot drop to the concrete sidewalk. I'm fifty-five years old, and I can still feel those arms around me.

Ellen had a second experience in her thirties. She was preparing to host a party and the clock was running down. With two children under the age of five and underfoot, it had taken her longer than she had anticipated to prepare the meal, set the table, shower, and get ready. She was doing the last of the dishes, standing at the kitchen sink. She took a moment to look out the window at the apricot tree just beyond the deck. It always made her smile. She noticed that her lower back was beginning to ache. She returned her attention to the dishes.

Moments later Ellen felt something like a string rubbing across the part of her back that was sore. It felt good. She assumed it was one of her children goofing around with her.

"Hey, what are you doing?" she said out loud, a smile in her voice.

She turned around. No one was there.

To this day, she believes it was her angels once again taking care of her; she had felt their touch.

⌒

I never even considered receiving personal oracles through the sense of smell until Cindy shared the following experiences.

Newly divorced after thirty-five years of marriage, Cindy was adjusting to being alone. During that transitional time, she became aware of an occasional strong scent in her home that she'd never noticed before. It was a sweet, somewhat smoky, almost pipelike tobacco smell. At first she thought it was residue from the fireplace, even though she noticed it in every room of the house. As time went by, she smelled the aroma no matter where she went—in her car, out shopping, in other people's homes.

Somewhere along the way Cindy started to connect the dots. The smell seemed to always be present when she felt the most alone and lonely. She even smelled it while trying to figure out how to complete a chore that her husband had always done. The scent never annoyed her. It was just the opposite. It soothed her soul at a very deep level. As the scent continued to follow her everywhere and show up when she needed support, it dawned on her that it was the essence of her father, who had died seventeen years earlier. From then on, every time she smelled the familiar smell, she could feel him encouraging and supporting her, and providing comfort.

Cindy got remarried, to Wally, a journalist who had an open and curious mind. She asked her new husband if he had ever noticed a certain scent in the air. He had and described it as the same smoky, wooded aroma she'd been experiencing. Wally had noticed the smell at times when he needed support, as well, and he had already identified it as the presence of his father. Cindy was blown away—she and her husband, independent of each other, had interpreted the scent as the spiritual presence of their own fathers. Cindy and Wally delighted in being able to share with each other their powerful and comforting connection with their fathers.

As this phenomenon continued, they mentioned their experiences to several family members. Cindy's mother and one of her sisters revealed that they, too, had noticed the same aroma at certain times. Up to that point, however, the women had not identified the scent with anything in particular, but the feeling of it being "Daddy's presence" quickly resonated with them.

A short time later, Wally was visiting his son who had moved to a new city when out of the blue his son remarked, "Have you noticed that from time to time this whole town seems to smell like barbecue?" The son had no clue what the other family members were experiencing, or that his grandfather was with him giving him an assist from the other side.

Cindy's father's healing presence popped up again some years later when she was visiting her mother and sister in Colorado. One morning her sister delved into an emotional issue involving their parents that had plagued her since childhood. The sister was talking when Cindy became aware of the scent of their father. As the sister's emotions intensified, the scent grew stronger. Cindy asked her sister to stop. She pointed out the smell and told her sister that Daddy was near and reassuring them that everything was okay. They could move beyond the emotional hurt. The sisters hugged and cried. Cindy's sister was finally able to release her emotional hold on an issue that had burdened her for years.

It's heartwarming to know that spirits of deceased family members can still support us and even help us heal issues from the past. Just imagine if everyone had been experiencing the smell but no one mentioned it or connected the dots and recognized it as the essence of their fathers. The evidence of the fathers' "there-ness" might have been disregarded and the potential for comfort and healing would have been missed.

In case you're wondering, neither father smoked a pipe. Cindy called it when she said, "I know it's a leap to 'know' the smoky, sweet scent we smell is the presence of our fathers, but it's just that . . . we 'know.'" Decoding your personal oracles is all about making that leap of faith. Chances are it will be validated further on down the line.

Sometimes recognizing a personal oracle is as simple as learning about someone else's experiences, as it was for me in this case.

After our beloved dog Pandora passed, I noticed a trace of her scent in her favorite place, the kitchen seating area where she had spent the most time with us. In the last months of her life a skin condition resulted in open wounds that gave her the scent of dried blood. That might sound terrible to some, but for me it was the opposite. I was so grateful for every bit of time we had with her that I grew to love that smell as evidence of her presence. On the twenty-fourth night after she passed, I tucked the covers under my chin and noticed the same sweet Pandora scent, now in my bedroom. My rational mind piped in to suggest the smell was transferring from my pajamas or bedclothes. But I had just laundered my husband's nightclothes and mine, and had changed our sheets the day before. Although Pandora had always been a welcome snuggler in our bed, in the last months of her life she was too weak to make it up the flights of stairs to our newly remodeled upstairs and onto our new mattress.

Would I have recognized Pandora's scent as a sign of her continuing presence even if Cindy and Wally hadn't shared their experiences with the scent of her father? I hope so.

ANIMALS

> In the beginning of all things, wisdom and knowledge were with the animals, for Tuawa, the one above, did not speak directly to man. He sent animals to tell man that he showed himself through the beasts and that from them, and from the stars and the sun, and moon, man should learn . . . for all things speak of Tuawa.
>
> —PAWNEE INDIAN CHIEF LETAKOS-LESA

Throughout history, animals have had special symbolic meanings associated with them. The lion is well known for his ferocity and his role as guardian—protector of the door to palaces and cathedrals. The lamb is a symbol of innocence and vulnerability. The lamb lying with the lion represents a state of peace. Even Napoleon chose to embellish his official emblems with two eagles, signifying his power and strength, along with bees to symbolize immortality.

The Native American culture understands the connection that exists between humans and animals, a connection capable of drawing together a specific human and a specific animal at a precise moment. Native Americans further believe that an animal consciously offers its body as food to a particular human or group of humans. This interconnection highlights how the timely appearance of an animal can serve as a personal oracle. I could write an entire book about animals as personal oracles, but for now, here are some stories to illustrate the different ways the animal kingdom might deliver personal oracles to you.

My son, David, had just started a new business when he had an accident that required extensive surgery to rebuild his face. Though uneasy about taking four weeks off to recuperate from surgery, he had no choice. As the pain and swelling in his eyes receded, he contracted a serious case of cabin fever. That's when he and I set off for his favorite Colorado stream for a hearty, healing dose of nature.

We sat quietly listening to the burbling water, inspired by the tenacity of plants peeking out of tiny rock crevices and thriving with no visible soil to nurture their roots. The energy was magical. Nothing specific happened, however, until we made our way back up the side of the canyon. David put his hand on my shoulder and whispered, "Mom, look, over there. A squirrel's tucked in beside that rock." The squirrel sat tight as we paused to look at it and wonder about the message it was delivering.

Back at home, we consulted the book *Medicine Cards* by Jamie Sams and David Carson and were reminded that a squirrel prepares for the scarcity of winter by gathering a plentiful supply of nuts in advance. David had done just that. During the time between his accident and the surgery to repair his face, he had worked diligently to ensure that his customers were well taken care of until he was able to return to work. The appearance of this little squirrel offered David validation for a job well done and gave him permission to rest and allow his body to heal.

When researching the significance of a specific animal messenger and considering the vast number of possible interpretations, always pay attention to what resonates with you personally and what is occurring in your life at the time. Remember, when it comes to interpreting personal oracles it's important to note that the same symbol or animal can represent totally different things to each individual. Watch what happened with the next group of women when they were visited by a snake.

During a personal oracle workshop at my home in Arizona, Annie shared some amazing synchronicities that had recently reconnected her with the parents of one of her closest childhood friends, who had died at age eighteen. She hadn't seen them since her friend's funeral. Annie was right in the middle of her story when a couple of the women gasped. They looked like they were ready to jump out of their skin. They had spotted a snake coiled tightly around a patio chair. It peered at the group through the closed glass door. Needless to say, all attention shifted to the snake. Some were fascinated, others were frightened, but no one could take their eyes off this unexpected visitor. In time we settled down and then began sharing our personal interpretations of what this snake's appearance signified to each of us.

Annie interpreted the snake as a conduit for the spirit of her deceased friend, letting her know he was right there with her.

Jo Searles, a retired Penn State professor with a penchant for discovering hidden messages, and an affinity for snakes, spoke up. Searles started out by saying that her experiences with snakes as personal oracles had always tended toward transformation. She went on to explain that before a snake sheds its skin, its eyes cloud over, which indicates it is entering the stage between life and death. Moving between the states of healing and enlightenment. She interpreted the arrival of this snake as a positive confirmation of her retirement, a sign that she was rebirthing into a new stage in her life. The old skin represented her life as a professor. What lay ahead for her was freedom—and with that freedom an expansion of her creativity and wisdom.

Pamela, who had been sitting with her back to the glass door, was petrified. The mere thought of snakes made her skin crawl, let alone seeing one up close and personal. She was terrified that it might make its way through the glass door and attack her. For her, the snake represented fear for her own safety.

Note that this particular snake offered three quite different personal oracle messages. Is one right or better than the rest? Absolutely not. They are all valid, because each message resonates to a specific individual. It's easy to fall into patterns of restrictive thinking and assume personal oracles are either all black or all white, that they hold only one message for everyone. But in reality, they are like a rainbow of colors; every color speaks uniquely to each individual. Here's another example of what I'm talking about.

I felt honored and blessed by the three owls that for months had faithfully perched in or under the tree outside my office and was eager to point them out to author and friend Gregg McNamee when he arrived for a meeting. He and I observed the little owls sitting quietly on the ground with their eyes closed. Our discussion expanded into the many myths and mysteries associated with owl energy. The owl sees into the darkness. It is a keeper of sacred knowledge and offers protection, intelligence, and support during times of transition. For me, the owls validated the divine wisdom and mystery supporting my work. Gregg offered his own contrasting owl experience.

It was a dark night when he and his mother embarked on an emergency road trip to the bedside of his gravely ill grandfather. Out of the darkness, an owl swooped directly toward the windshield. At the last moment, the bird pulled up to avoid crashing into the glass. Gregg and his mother's shock turned to dread. According to their Native American ancestry, the owl represents death. Like the grim reaper, it accompanies spirits from this world to the next. Sadly, Gregg's grandfather did pass a short time later.

There is something extraordinary about the next animal story and the accompanying photo. I stumbled across it one night when I was watching the ABC show *20/20*.

Reporter-photographer Kimberly Launier describes it as "a simple *20/20* shoot [that] turned into something that made me wonder about life after death. I was filming soldier Justin Rollins's parents, Skip and Rhonda, playing with their dog, Hero, whose rescue from the Iraq War zone where Justin died was nothing short of a miracle."

It all started the night before a roadside bomb killed Justin Rollins, when he completed one final heroic act; he saved an abandoned puppy. The army fulfilled the Rollinses' request to bring the dog home from the war zone so that they could hold onto a living piece of their fallen son. They named the dog Hero.

"Sometimes when Rhonda hugged Hero she would pet her face softly and coo, 'Justin, are you in there?' It was Rhonda's

Kimberly Launier / ABC News

gentle way of remembering their son and his last living connection to Hero. At one point, Hero wandered off and took a stroll in the backyard. All of a sudden, the clouds broke and a light began to solidify in a beam directly down on Hero—a kind of vertical halo.

"As this dramatic ray of light was shining on Hero, she turned to look at me, and it was all I could do to hold the camera steady and not drop it in astonishment. It was an unforgettable moment, and made me wonder if in fact Justin was in there. Then the light vanished."

Kimberly couldn't wait to check her camera's playback to see if it had caught the stunning beam. When she saw that it did, she was so happy she burst out dancing. She says it was a great moment to share with Justin's parents. They all laughed together. Everyone felt like they had witnessed a sign from Justin. What do you think?

EARTH WHISPERS

Mother Earth whispers personal oracles through all forms of nature. Take the Taos turtle that instructed me to slow down and Georgia's tree that symbolized the balance missing in her life. Or the simple guidance from a cloud that cast a shadow of a bat on the mountain just outside my office window one day. I knew from previous encounters that bat energy symbolizes change. The image of the shadow bat was signaling me to embrace the changes occurring in my work as it evolved and encouraging me to continue to trust the universe to guide the way.

If you're a city dweller, the idea of Spirit speaking through nature may conjure up images that require quiet and solitude in the woods. I can assure you that's not always the case. My husband, Kenneth, and I were walking from the Royal Horseguards hotel in the center of London to Charing Cross train station when a shape on the sidewalk drew my attention like a magnet. There at my feet, in the middle of the bustling sidewalk, lay a perfectly formed image of a heart. I squatted down to examine it. The morning rains had evaporated from the cement, allowing the elements of nature to combine and form a perfectly defined heart. It felt like nature was imprinting a sidewalk tattoo of the love energy that surrounded the family wedding we had just attended. It was like finding a lucky penny from heaven—no, make that a jar full of pennies. I snapped a photo of it. To this day, the London heart remains pinned to my bulletin board. A reminder that love and luck sometimes sit right in front of us, and that universal love is with us all the way.

Over the years the London sidewalk heart has served as a personal oracle for many different people. When I share the image
in workshops, the twig in the "heart of the heart" often becomes
a center of focus. Some have interpreted the graceful form as
a twig-shaped goddess with her arms outstretched and her
head turned ever so slightly to the right. Others identified the
twig as a tiny angel with wings. A young girl saw a fairy-
shaped image and suggested that it might be a gift from the fairy
realm.

Sherice, who was struggling to put the pieces of her marriage back together after her husband's infidelity, found comfort by imagining herself as the graceful twig tucked safely inside the heart. She placed the photograph in a frame and set it on her bedside table. Each night before going to sleep, she would close her eyes and imagine herself as the indomitable center image. Eventually Sherice did become that strong, graceful woman with her arms outstretched and her heart open.

Try tuning in to the London sidewalk heart for yourself. What do you see? How does it make you feel?

SONGS, BOOKS, AND THE WRITTEN WORD

Let's take a look at songs that delivered timely messages straight to these people's ears. Some are prophetic, some are just plain fun. You might say this first story is out of this world.

Liz showed up as usual that afternoon at the hospital, but found the room empty. Her good friend Steve had been in a coma for the past month as a result of a serious bicycle accident and Liz had been visiting him regularly. She would talk and joke, believing Steve could hear her, and give her friend massages and play CDs they had enjoyed listening to before the accident. One of their favorite songs was "Anytime" by Brian McKnight.

But today for the first time, Steve wasn't in his room. She didn't know whether to be hopeful or concerned.

"Excuse me," she said to a nurse, busy at a computer behind the desk. "Do you know where my friend in room 112 is?"

"Let's see," the nurse said, picking up a clipboard. "He was taken into surgery about an hour ago."

Liz frowned.

"The doctor discovered that the pressure in his brain had become dangerously high. She's performing emergency surgery to relieve it. He probably won't be back up here for quite a while. If you'd like to leave your phone number, I can call you when he returns."

Liz left her number and walked back to her car, expecting to retrace her steps before day's end. She had driven only two blocks when the song "Anytime" came on the radio. She started to cry. Not because she was worried about Steve or sad that they couldn't share the song together. The minute the song started, Liz knew that Steve had died.

She arrived home to find a message on her answering machine from the hospital, simply asking her to call.

"I'm so sorry to have to tell you this, Liz," the same nurse told her when she called. "Steve died during surgery."

"I had a feeling," said Liz. "By any chance was the time of death two thirty-five P.M.?"

Silence filled the phone. Then an incredulous voice said, "Yes. It was. How did you know?"

The song acted as their secret code. Others who were listening just heard a song. Not Liz. She knew in her gut she was receiving a signal from Steve that he was gone.

Like Liz, Randy was familiar with the song that delivered a message to him. In fact, he cranked up the volume every time he heard it on the radio. After all, who didn't know Van Halen? But he heard it with new ears on his son Sam's birthday. A group of college buddies had given Sam a parachute jump, complete with a bird's-eye video of the drop. They invited Randy to join the adventure. He had said no, but the boys' cajoling—"You gotta do it, man," and "We're all gonna jump"—wore him down. Randy agreed to go, but planned to catch the action from the ground with his video camera.

On Sam's birthday, the group piled in the family SUV. "You're gonna jump, right, Randy?" asked one of the guys. Randy had been rethinking his decision. He was tempted to try skydiving. Before he had time to answer, one of the kids turned on the radio and turned up the volume. David Lee Roth of Van Halen was belting out the chorus from his hit "Jump." "Might as well jump, Go ahead, jump, jump." No one in the car missed the significance of the song. By the time the last chorus rolled around, the boys were singing at the top of their lungs. Randy took the song's message to heart. You guessed it—he jumped and had the time of his life.

The guidance and problem-solving mystery of personal oracles lies hidden in books and all kinds of printed material. It could be a religious tome like the Bible, a book of poetry, or your favorite novel, history book, biography, or even the dictionary. Newspapers and magazines can offer guidance, as well.

Try this simple exercise. Use your internal guidance system to choose a book from your bookshelf or one on your e-reader. Open the book to a random page. Some people I know close their eyes, point to a place on the page, and read where their finger lands. I like to let my eyes fall where they may. Sometimes I even scan the entire page so I don't miss any hidden messages. You can

even do this with the morning newspaper or magazines in grocery store lines or waiting rooms. Be as specific as you want when
seeking guidance, or simply see what speaks to you and notice
how it relates to your life. Chances are you will receive insights
into your life and perhaps even some solutions worth putting
into action.

UNIVERSAL SYMBOLS AND NUMEROLOGY

Personal oracles often translate through symbols and numerology. Symbols work like metaphors. They flesh out a message or
articulate an idea. Symbols such as a heart and a rainbow are part
of a universal language that requires no explanation. Flash someone a thumbs-up anywhere around the world, and you'll probably get a concurring grin and an affirmative nod of the head. And
yet when these symbols appear in our life, they speak to our personal, individual circumstances.

Similarly, numerology is a really cool way of looking at
how the universe works with us. This ancient practice is like a
hidden secret code. Each number resonates a specific energy
that runs through everything. Another piece of the interconnected web of life is revealed when we take the time to learn
the code.

The dragon is considered to be a magical and protective energy
sacred to many cultures, including Tibetan, East Indian, and
Celtic. My friend Serfina became well acquainted with the dragon
symbol one day during 2012, the Year of the Dragon.

Since the last Year of the Dragon in 2000, I've wanted to get a dragon tattoo. For me, the dragon represents the creative life force, strength, courage, and the ability to manifest. So when 2012 came along, I decided it was time. In the morning of the day I was scheduled to get tattooed, I was watching the Weather Channel. Someone had sent in a cloud picture that was a perfectly clear dragon, complete with a highlighted red wing and red eye! I thought of my mother, who was born in the Year of the Dragon, and remembered I have dragon in my Chinese horoscope. As I was driving into town I was thinking about the importance of reclaiming my own dragon nature with this tattoo.

I stopped to fill up at my regular gas station, which always has U-Haul trucks with pictures on them. I'd been going there for years, but this was the first time I ever saw one with a dragonfly on it. I stopped at a light in town and saw a very distressed homeless guy and felt compelled to give him some money. As he came to get it, I saw he had a big dragon on his T-shirt. The final symbol appeared when I stopped at another light and turned my head to the left. I was directly in front of a tattoo shop with dragons all over the storefront. The sign read: "Tattooing—experience the dragon." I felt like I was getting a huge thumbs-up. They were all confirmations to me of the significance and deep meaning behind the ritual of getting this tattoo.

Following are two stories related to numbers. Numbers are not just mathematical symbols; they also embody mystical hidden meanings. The universal language of numerology speaks to us every day, from the date on the calendar to the time on the clock. But numbers deliver much more information—they deliver personal oracles, as mentioned above, and have been recognized as doing so for centuries. Pay attention to numbers that catch your attention. They may be signaling you to take another look and consider a message that is hiding in the code. When you feel like they might be sending a personal oracle your way, investigate their numerological meaning on the Internet or in books.

Let me set the stage for this first story about my friend Patricia and the number ninety-seven. Patricia and her husband, Stan, live on one hundred acres of open grassy land with an expansive panorama of the Arizona sky. One afternoon she was in the backyard when she noticed an exceptionally large flock of ravens approaching. As soon as she spotted them, she followed her instinct and started counting. They were flying so fast that she had difficulty doing so and wished they would slow down. The old saying "Your wish is my command" springs to mind, because the entire flock of ravens did just that; they slowed down. Patricia counted ninety-seven ravens.

I asked if that number had any particular meaning for her. "My mother died in 1997," Patricia said. She went on to share how her English-born mother had seeded her fascination with ravens. "When I was seven, we visited the Tower of London, and my mother told me about the legend of the ravens." The legend goes that if the ravens leave the Tower of London, England will fall from power. "The idea of ravens having such a mystical power fascinated me and made a lasting impression on me. Counting ninety-seven of them in the sky linked me to my mother and my original introduction to them and their magic."

Ravens are Patricia's spirit guides. For her as well as others, they are the sky messengers of the animal kingdom and possess prophetic powers. They fly with us to the higher realms of magic. Some refer to ravens as the Einsteins of the bird world—brilliant but smart enough to play. They were playing and delivering a message the day ninety-seven of them flew across Patricia's home.

⟋

After years of being unhappily married, Maggie Ann had reached her breaking point. The time had come to file for divorce. She hesitated, however, because she was dealing with graduate school classes and assignments, a full-time job, and three teenage boys, one of whom was going through some heavy-duty personal challenges. Her frustration and fatigue levels had risen to an all-time high. But more than anything, she knew she needed out of the relationship that undermined her self-worth and self-confidence.

After Maggie Ann filed, she began to notice that almost every time she looked at a clock, the number one or eleven appeared. She'd wake up in the middle of the night and the clock on her nightstand glowed a red 1:11 A.M. She'd pick up her phone to check for messages and it would be 11:11 A.M. She started writing down the times she saw the number—on a clock, a license plate, in a newspaper or a book. One week, she saw the number 1, 11, or 111 every single day. A friend suggested Maggie Ann consult the numerology chart in Ted Andrews's book *Animal Speak*. She did and felt her wounded heart open a bit when she read that the number one is a sign of new beginnings, just where she was headed! Her curiosity was piqued. She Googled "numerology significance of 11:11" and up popped an entire page on Wikipedia: "Numerologists believe that events linked to the time 11:11 appear more often than can be explained by chance or coincidence. This belief is related to the concept of synchronicity. Some claim that seeing 11:11 is an auspicious sign. Others claim that 11:11 signals spirit presence." Another source suggested that she was being instructed to keep her thoughts positive because they would be manifesting quickly. From then on, Maggie Ann felt comfort and encouragement every time she saw those numbers. She felt like a higher power was watching out for her.

Universal signs and symbols can pop up everywhere. The symbol for peace worked its magic for me the day I was driving and thinking about a friend's comment during a recent conversation. She had said, "You're giving her the benefit of the doubt." As I thought about this, a complementary quote from my friend Judy's father popped into my mind. "I'd rather think the best of someone and be wrong," he said, "than think the worst of someone and be wrong." While waiting at the next stoplight, I glanced at the car beside me and noticed the very specific position of the driver's arm. He had wedged his elbow, forearm, and two fingers between the bottom and the top of his window. His index finger and middle finger pointed up and formed a perfect peace sign. The synchronicity of my thoughts combined with sighting this sign at that precise moment sent a clear message to me. The divine mystery seemed to be agreeing that our world would be more peaceful if we all gave each other the benefit of the doubt.

MEMORY IMPRINTS AND SEEDS
OF OUR ANCESTORS

Memory imprints and seeds of our ancestors are like secret codes embedded in our cells, much like strands of DNA. They help shape the lenses through which we view life, and influence our everyday experiences. Some memory imprints originate during childhood. All the years I spent looking for shapes and images in absolutely everything imprinted in me a certain way of relating to life. The trip to the Tower of London with her English-born mother implanted in seven-year-old Patricia a sense of awe and reverence for ravens, who later became her spirit guides. Many of the people who notice significant messages in license plates grew up in families that made a game out of spotting unusual license plates. Memory imprints also can occur during adulthood, like the favorite song Liz and her friend shared. Seeds of our ancestors, on the other hand, are embedded in our cellular consciousness. My Native American perspective that all of life is interconnected and sacred was not taught to me, the way identifying images was taught. It resonates from a deep level of *knowing*. Both memory imprints and seeds of our ancestors influence us on an unconscious level. Becoming conscious of them can offer clues to why our personal oracles resonate with us the way they do.

Some of my fondest memory imprints are of our family gathered around a crackling fire burning in Grandma Mason's welcoming fireplace. Like the fire ceremonies of our ancestors, we would snuggle down in our blankets, settle in, and gaze into the flames.

Like a crowd watching fireworks, we would ooh and aah as flames crackled and popped and morphed into recognizable shapes. Then, later in the evening, when only the embers remained, we would share the mysterious images we had discovered hidden within the embers. I remember spotting angels and birds with wings fluttering. I especially loved discovering deep, mysterious tunnels that burned through the logs and were lined with embers that glistened like fairy lights. The boys saw snakes. I don't remember any personal oracles, but it was like boot camp—training me for what was to come.

This magical fireplace was tucked neatly between two crisp white bookcases. Inside their shining glass doors sat my grandmother's most treasured books. The books all looked interesting, but a heavy gunmetal bookend fascinated me the most. It had a sense of presence, with impressive pillars on either side of a large piece of slate. You had to hold it in the light to read the embossed words and see the image of the wise-looking bearded man, William Cullen Bryant, who sat proudly above his words "Go forth, under the open sky, and list / To Nature's teachings," from the poem "Thanatopsis." This memory imprint planted seeds of awareness in my soul, and impressed upon me at a young age that I could commune with and learn from nature.

⌣

Cynthia was about ten years old the first time she saw an airplane pulling a message banner behind it. She remembers squealing with glee as the small airplane flew above the ocean in front of the crowd gathered on the sandy beach. The banner read "Happy Birthday, Jan. We Love You." She didn't know Jan, but she thought Jan was the luckiest person on earth.

Over the years, Cynthia saw other banners flying above the ocean but none with a message for her. That is, until she became a midwife and received a series of banner messages. She was driving in her car on the way to deliver a baby when a mystical airplane pulling a banner message flew in front of her mind's eye. The one-word banner read "Hemorrhage." Later, during the birth of that baby, the mother did in fact hemorrhage, but Cynthia had been forewarned, so she was able to quickly control the excessive bleeding. The second birth-related banner read "Placenta." This new mother had a difficult time releasing the placenta. Again all went well. Cynthia had received a heads-up. The third banner had nothing to do with birthing babies. It arrived when she was having an urge to relocate. This banner read "Tucson." Her previous experiences with these prophetic messages had been right on target, so Cynthia packed up her things and off she went to Tucson. That banner proved to be right on target, as well. Cynthia loves Tucson and has not an ounce of regret about moving.

CLEDONS

Have you ever heard of cledons? The word may be new to you, but chances are you've experienced them. Cledons are those statements you overhear that give you the perfect answer to something that's going on in your life at the time. Let's say you're standing in line at the supermarket thinking about a difficult family situation. Maybe your parents are aging, and you've done all you can do to help them, but your siblings want you to do even more. That's when you hear the person behind you say into her cell phone, "Just give it up—there's nothing more you can do." The

ANN BOLINGER-McQUADE

moment you hear those words, you know they ring true for you—you can let go of worry and the need to do more.

Tamara shared a story with me about the time she had an urge to go shopping in the Taos Ski Valley. What she really needed to do was stock the pantry with food for her and her son, not browse shops for things she didn't need. Tamara detoured into a favorite clothing store and was chatting with the clerk when the phone rang. It was the owner checking in. Tamara wanted to finish their conversation, so she wandered over to a display of sweaters. She couldn't help tuning in to the clerk's description of how she could walk and stand with less pain. The last few weeks of her Feldenkrais classes coupled with her Qigong exercises had taught her how to work with her body to manage chronic back pain.

A bell went off in Tamara's mind. Her son Michael's back was a mess. He had missed a considerable amount of school and was going to miss the entire ski season. The doctors claimed back surgery was the only recourse. Suddenly, she understood why she was at the Ski Valley in that particular shop. Tamara left the shop clutching a piece of paper with the phone number for the Feldenkrais classes and the word "Qigong" scribbled beside it. She didn't have a new sweater, but she had new hope for her son.

Hopefully you've noticed that personal oracles translate through every form imaginable. It all depends on the tailor-made delivery system that's intended for you. They can be delivered through clouds, animals or nature, universal symbols, or those mysterious cledons and random words that appear out of nowhere, or anything else designed to catch your attention. The universe is always on standby, ready to interact with us.

96

Remember not to discount anything. Nothing is too strange, too unreal, or too impossible. Whether our messages respond to a request, surprise us, or we go scouting for them, one thing you can count on is that every personal oracle is responding to a need—your need. That's the beauty of personal oracles.

Personal oracles are everyday miracles that often go unnoticed. But when we know what to look for, they offer firsthand experience of the invisible threads that link everything in our universe. My desk dictionary defines a miracle as "an extraordinary or unusual event that is considered to be a manifestation of divine or supernatural powers, something that excites admiration, awe, or wonder." The more we explore the miracles of everyday personal oracles, the more we experience the supernatural as the natural order of things. In his book *Miracles*, C. S. Lewis suggests that "miracles do not break the laws of nature; miracles are the law of nature." Personal oracles are those miracles delivered directly to your door.

Chapter 5

Sharpening Your Sixth Sense
Tuning In to Hidden Messages

*It is always with excitement that I wake up in the
morning wondering what my intuition will toss
up to me, like gifts from the sea. I work with it
and rely on it. It's my partner.*

—Jonas Salk

Let's talk intuition, that sixth sense that is sometimes referred to as innate knowledge, ESP, gut reaction, hunch, and clairvoyance. Think of intuition as the gentle whisper of knowing that often defies reason. It often hovers right below the surface of our awareness. It's the sense that nudges us to take a sweater even though the sun is shining or to call a distant friend for no apparent reason other than to say hello. When the shifting wind delivers chilly air or we discover our friend needs emotional support, we're thankful for our intuition. Most of us use it every day without giving it a second thought.

When it comes to tuning in to personal oracles, this sense takes first place. The question is: How do we recognize and sharpen our intuition?

RECOGNIZING YOUR INTUITION

I have to credit my aunt Evie for introducing me to the power of intuition.

Her story alone would have intrigued me, but when she sat me down at her kitchen table and stared purposefully into my eyes, I knew she was going to share something important. What I didn't know was that her words would impact me for the rest of my life.

She proceeded to tell me about the day she was out and about running errands and was overcome by an urgent feeling to return home. When she opened the front door, the telephone's incessant ringing greeted her. A police dispatcher informed her that her husband had been in a head-on collision and was being rushed to the nearby hospital in critical condition. Tears welled up in her eyes as she recalled the moment when her car and the ambulance pulled into the emergency entrance at the same time. I envisioned her walking alongside the gurney, her hand on my unconscious uncle's arm, then keeping vigil in the intensive care unit until the crisis passed. She went on to say how thankful she was that she had listened to her intuition that day, and how she promised herself never to ignore it again. I still can feel the intensity of her gaze when she said, "Ann, always trust your intuition." From that day on, I followed her advice. Through the years I have experienced the rich nuances of intuition that have guided and saved me in more ways than I can count or even recall.

The way we experience intuition is as unique as the way we experience personal oracles. It can stream into us in a variety of ways. Your intuition, for instance, may communicate through a warm or noticeable feeling in your gut, or a subtle energetic tug somewhere in your body that lets you know when something significant is occurring. Or it may translate through a deep-seated sense of knowing that some describe as a feeling in their bones. Maybe you've experienced your intuition as the sensation of goose bumps on your skin, or perhaps as a thought or image flashing through your mind, or the sound of a voice telling you something.

These are six ways your intuition can communicate with you:

- Clairvoyance
- Clairaudience
- Clairsentience
- Clairolfactory
- Claircognizance
- Telepathy

As you read through these stories, pay attention to which ones resonate with you. Perhaps you've already experienced one or all of them. Furthermore, you may recall some of your own intuitive hits and experiences. Give yourself permission to access these memories. Invite them to float into your consciousness, and then, if you're so inclined, record them in a journal. You may discover a pattern of how you interact with your intuition. Note that the prefix *clair* in most of the terms discussed means "clear" in French.

CLAIRVOYANCE

Clairvoyance translates to "clear seeing." This occurs when our mind's eye sees symbols or pictures. If you're a visual person, you already may be thinking in images. These images might flash across the mind's screen for no more than a second or two. The image of a birthday cake with your friend blowing out her candles might flash across your mind's screen as a reminder of her upcoming birthday. Or your mind's eye might see significant words on a banner alerting you to something that is coming your way. Take note of images that seem to appear randomly; they could be your intuition speaking to you, offering guidance and support of all kinds.

Some clairvoyants see images that other people don't see. Annick, for instance, has been seeing spirits from other dimensions for as along as she can remember. At age seventeen, she worked as a waitress to put herself through nursing school. One afternoon she saw four people walk through the restaurant's door and sit at a table that was clean but not yet set. Annick retrieved silverware and napkins and placed one set in front of each person. One of the women picked up the napkin and cutlery in front of one chair and handed them back to Annick. "There are only three of us," she said. No one but Annick saw the friend who had joined them from the other side.

As you can imagine, with this kind of "sight," Annick has witnessed many happenings via the spirit world. Her nursing career has brought her to the bedside of many people in transition through the death process. Almost every time she sees a spirit leave its body, it exits through the top of the head. Except once. Much to her surprise, the spirit exited through the solar plexus. Her reaction: "I guess it happens that way, too."

CLAIRAUDIENCE

If you've experienced "clear hearing," you most likely have heard distinct words in your head or maybe just outside your ear. Remember Rhonda and the hummingbird? She heard the word "danger" on the outside of her left ear. And Alan, the pilot who seeded clouds over his ranch? He heard a mysterious voice repeat a warning as clearly as if someone were speaking to him from a few feet away. That same voice spoke to Alan one other time, and again, Alan ended up heeding its advice.

When Alan's father became too ill to run the family ranch, he passed the management reins to his son. Though they loved each other, they had always been at odds about how the business should be run. Years passed, and the cattle business became more competitive, incorporating new methods of breeding cattle in an attempt to maximize resources. Over the years Alan consulted with his father about using these new methods, but each time he met with such resistance that he stopped telling his father what he was up to. Their cattle business thrived. Then one day Alan heard that same voice. *"Show your father what you've done."* Alan shrugged it off. No way was he going to confront his father again. After all, his condition was deteriorating almost daily by then.

But the voice persisted. *"Show your father what you've done."* Finally, he gave in. He went to the house and helped his father walk down to the corrals. Alan drove his father around, pointing out some of the changes he had made and explaining why and how they all came about. His father watched and listened intently, his steely resistance transforming to awe and respect. "You've done a great job, son," he said. Alan's heart warmed. His father's words were like a salve to the frustration and pain he often had felt from rarely receiving acknowledgment for jobs well done.

When Alan woke the next morning, he discovered that his father had died in his sleep during the night. He grieved his father's passing, but at the same time he felt grateful to the voice for speaking, and what's more, for speaking until he paid attention.

CLAIRSENTIENCE

People who are clairsentient "feel" their intuition. It might be a tingling or warmth in part of their body such as their stomach, hence the term "gut feeling," or maybe a twitch of a finger, mouth, or eyelid. My friend Karen, for example, experiences her intuition as a prickly, tingling sensation in her scalp.

While sweeping the floor after dinner one evening, Karen noticed that familiar itchy feeling ringing the crown of her head. She thought it odd. Usually something like a conversation, an idea, or an image triggered the sensation. This time the tingling started spontaneously. She decided to pay extra attention to what she was doing, which was sweeping the kitchen floor. Five strokes later, she just about freaked out. In the middle of the floor sat a translucent bark scorpion. Its light-colored shell blended into the tile. Bark scorpions sting with venom particularly harmful to young children and those with compromised immune systems, like her husband. The entire family had been walking around barefoot for hours.

I'm forever grateful that my husband, Kenneth, acted on his gut feeling the night we met more than thirty years ago. It was one of those blind dates arranged by a friend who had been trying to get us together for a couple of years. Anyone who has ever been on a blind date knows how uncomfortable they can be, and this one was no different.

Throughout dinner, this English gentleman from the corporate world and I—a single mother of three, making her way in the fashion industry—struggled to find common ground. When we finally stepped onto the dance floor, all awkwardness vanished. We had been dancing for some time, my head nestled against Kenneth's shoulder, when my neck began to cramp. I was reluctant to move and break the magic. The very next moment, I felt Kenneth's warm hand. To my amazement, he began to massage the very points on the back of my neck that hurt. I wasn't sure whether this man was psychic or a wizard, but I felt sure that this was no coincidence.

Weeks later, I asked him how he knew my neck hurt, and he said that he didn't know. He just followed a gut feeling to rub it. For me, the experience was a personal oracle signaling a unique connection between this man and me. From that point on, there was no turning back for either of us.

CLAIROLFACTORY

As you may have guessed, clairolfactory refers to "clear smell." I've yet to meet a person who describes themselves as clairolfactory. But intuitive hits involving scents and aromas happen more often than we might realize, as Cindy and Wally can attest.

Esperanza sat across from the medium. During previous sessions with this medium, she had received incredible messages from the other side. Though she was open to receiving what-ever messages filtered through that day, she secretly hoped the medium would connect with her father, who had been gone for decades, or her mother, who had passed on two years ago, or her lover, who had passed on earlier in the year.

The medium started by describing a scent she smelled in the room. It reminded her of the clean, fresh aroma you smell when you hug someone with newly washed hair. It had a hint of rose-mary and peppermint, too. Though Esperanza's nose didn't detect the scent, she knew it. Her lover had had the most gorgeous, silky, long, dark hair, which he washed and conditioned every day. Most of the time, he used a shampoo with rosemary in it. Esperanza loved to touch Sammy's soft hair and bury her nose in it. The medium told Esperanza that Sammy wanted her to know he was by her side more than she knew.

A few days later, while organizing boxes in the storage sec-tion of the garage, Esperanza noticed an unmistakable aroma. Tears welled up in her eyes. It was almost like hugging Sammy and burrowing her nose in his beautiful mane of freshly washed hair. Esperanza would never have categorized herself as clairol-factory, but the medium had put her intuition on alert, and now here she was experiencing the essence of her lover.

CLAIRCOGNIZANCE

Claircognizance, or "clear knowing," is a total understanding that occurs in a flash. It's that feeling of certainty, that download of knowingness that seems to appear out of thin air. Here are some examples of people who experienced intuition in this way.

As you will read, this knowing often turns out to be a premonition that comes true.

Samantha and her husband, Mark, rented a car when they arrived in Madrid. They headed toward their hotel, a slow journey in the stop-and-go city traffic. As Mark slowed down for a red light, the thought flashed through Samantha's mind to lock the car doors. She told Mark to hit the lock button. Not more than a minute later, two young men rushed up to their car and tried to open the doors, probably with the intent of robbing them.

⌐

The first thing that Kathryne thought of when she woke up Saturday morning was that she and Deana needed to go see a movie. Deana's health had been getting progressively worse. Only thirty-three years old and the mother of five boys, she suffered from a degenerative heart condition. Kathryne phoned Deana and made arrangements to pick her up. The two women spent a wonderful four hours together, just the two of them, a rare treat for Deana, who couldn't get out often, much less without children in tow. Two nights later, Deana's heart stopped working, and within a week she had passed. Kathryne forever will be grateful that she followed the guidance of her intuition.

⌐

Patty and her husband had been thinking about relocating from their home in the Midwest to a warmer climate. They visited Albuquerque, Santa Fe, Phoenix, Sedona, and Tucson. She was at a Hampton Inn in Tucson at two A.M. when she awoke from a sound sleep and bolted up in bed bathed in "knowing" where they would move. Even though they had not yet discussed which option would suit their family best, she just knew it would be Tucson. And she was right. Eight months later her husband received a job offer. They sold their house, packed up their furnishings, and with their kids and cat moved the two thousand miles to Arizona.

TELEPATHY

Telepathy is a type of psychic communication between two minds. Think of it as a type of automatic thought transference. It's that sense you get that the driver next to you is about to change lanes and you move over a moment before he merges. Or it's when good friends and couples finish each other's sentences or start talking about exactly what the other person had been thinking about.

Many children come into this world with their intuition fresh and activated. Veronica tells a story about her two-year-old daughter sitting in her high chair eating a Popsicle. Veronica was cleaning up the kitchen and thinking about two acquaintances, both named Barbara, and how she had confused them earlier in the day. All of a sudden little Hannah looked her in the eye and said, "Barbara." Veronica hadn't uttered a single thought out loud, much less the name Barbara. As a rule, children seem to have pretty open and clear channels of intuition, including telepathy.

Telepathic exchanges that occur between humans and animals also are commonplace. For his book *Dogs That Know When Their Owners Are Coming Home*, English scientist Rupert Sheldrake studied the telepathic connection between humans and dogs. He and his team performed experiment after experiment monitoring the behavior of the animal left at home as it related to its human companion who was away from home. Each time the human decided (set their intention) to return home, the dog moved to the place where he routinely greeted his human. They particularly noted that the reaction wasn't triggered when the humans approached their homes—it was triggered at the moment they decided to return home!

I've experienced more telepathic communications than I can recall. But this one changed my life forever. It occurred at a mall on the day before Christmas, while I was awaiting the test results of my breast cancer lumpectomy. I had a sudden urge to pop into a pet shop and admire the birds. My feet had barely crossed the threshold when I heard this matter-of-fact statement spoken directly into my left ear: *"You know I'm going home with you, don't you?"*

Startled, I glanced to my left. No one was there. Bewildered, I looked around to see who was talking; no one was nearby. I didn't have time to be alarmed or even consider what was going on; my attention went directly to a cage with three golden retriever puppies flip-flopping all over each other. One puppy drew me to him like a magnet. Mesmerized, I walked over to the cage to take a closer look, forgetting all about the birds—and even the mysterious words. A salesclerk came by and I asked to hold the puppy.

Kenneth walked in the store and saw me with the puppy now asleep and nestled comfortably in my arms. Instantly besotted, Kenneth made me an offer I immediately refused. "He's yours if you want him. He can be your Christmas present." Those words jerked me up short. What was going on? I was just having fun. I had absolutely no intention of taking this puppy home. I back-pedaled as fast as I could, handing the puppy back to the sales-clerk and saying we needed to leave and talk it over, though I had no intention of coming back to get him. Kenneth agreed, albeit reluctantly. He gave the tiny guy a gentle pat, then leaned over to kiss him on the top of his head and whisper something to him that I didn't hear: "Don't worry. I'll be right back to get you."

We walked back out into the mall. I resumed my last-minute shopping. At some point I realized Kenneth had disappeared. I retraced our steps to the pet shop. There was my husband, standing at the counter cradling the little puppy safely in his left arm like he was a treasure. His extended right hand held a credit card. A collar, leash, bowl, and other puppy "necessities" were piled on the counter.

Looking back, I'm amazed I didn't tell Kenneth about those prophetic words, especially since nothing like that had ever happened to me before. I didn't consciously discount the message; it just seemed to slip away due to everything else that was going on. Kenneth acted out the message without being aware of what the little puppy had predicted. Fortunately, he followed what his gut was telling him, and it changed my life for the better.

Rusty became my constant companion and beloved spirit guide. We were inseparable. He and I communicated telepathically, like most humans and their animals do, for the next eleven years. But I never heard his voice again until the day after he passed. That's when I received an even more astonishing message from him.

I woke up filled with dread, remembering that he had died, and started to sob quietly to myself. I lay there feeling lost, wondering what I would ever do without my Rusty Bear. Then I heard his voice, just as I had in the pet shop. *"I'm still here."* He paused— then came an offer that shocked and mystified me. *"I could come back if you want me to."* My sense of emptiness transformed instantly into joy and wonder. I immediately accepted his offer—this time with total trust and without hesitation.

I had never heard of anything like this and had no idea how it could happen. Luckily I didn't need to, thanks to timely conversations with strangers in restaurants and parking lots. They all shared their own scenarios of how their pets had returned to them, and every account was unique. Soon the idea of Rusty returning was not as strange as it sounded. I learned that Rusty wasn't the only animal returning to a loved one!

Other mysterious messages and significant images kept popping up everywhere, like a road map with hidden clues designed to lead me straight to him. I felt as if I had been hurled onto an invisible moving sidewalk that was transporting me safely through a portal and into another dimension of our shared world. Within this dimension was the reassurance and guidance I needed to assuage my fear of dying.

In the following fifty-seven days (a friend pointed out that is the gestation period for dogs), while the universe was guiding me back to Rusty, his spirit was coming full circle, from the death of his physical body to the essence of his spirit, and back into physical form. Rusty, our spirit guide, scouted ahead and returned to let us know, *"There is no death, only a change of worlds."* It is safe to travel beyond the veil into the unknown.

TRUSTING YOUR INTUITION

Muna shut the car door, turned the key in her ignition, and heaved a sigh of relief, happy to have completed her last errand. She would be home in ten minutes. At the stoplight, she glanced at the natural food market on the corner, one of her favorite stomping grounds, and had a sudden craving for carrot juice. Muna considered stopping to buy some, which also would give her a chance to stock up on cat food. But it had been a long day, and she was running low on energy. The thought of kicking off her shoes and slipping into her jammies spurred her on. She bypassed the store but didn't lose her craving for carrot juice. Later that night, wishing she had bought the carrot juice, Muna went to refill her kitty's bowl and discovered there was no cat food in the pantry.

Then there's the man who registered on this thought as it flashed through his mind: *Keeping your glasses in the case on your belt isn't a safe place for them.* He ignored the advice. If you guessed the glasses disappeared a few minutes later, you're right. He still kicks himself for losing the expensive prescription eyeglasses with his favorite frames that were no longer available.

Like Muna and our man with the missing eyeglasses, we all have stories of ignoring our intuition. Even though I took Aunt Evie's advice to heart, I, too, have disregarded my share of intuitive hits and wish that I could rewind and replay events, this time heeding the guidance given. Rather than kick ourselves, we need to ask what makes us ignore or not trust our intuition. Why do we dismiss it, shove it aside, or bypass it, especially when it offers such sage and timely advice?

The answer: monkey mind chatter.

Let me explain. Think of yourself as a giant radio receiver and transmitter with no off switch. You are hardwired to receive and send messages that connect you with the frequencies of other dimensions. This information flows back and forth through the

Divine Matrix of energy that connects us with everything in the entire universe. "The Divine Matrix" is a term author Gregg Braden uses to describe the tightly woven energetic web that extends through all creation. The information translates through your frequency of *knowing*, which is always on. (Think of it as a station on your car radio that broadcasts intuitive messages.) Then, of course, you have to trust those messages.

Right about now your mind may start yammering at you, thoughts like *What the heck is she talking about?* or *Invisible frequencies that connect us—what a bunch of hooey.* This is your monkey mind, and it's chattering up a storm because it doesn't like being pulled out of conventional, rational thinking. Well, here's your chance to take control. Switch off that channel of chatter and think about invisible frequencies that you use every day. Radio, television, and cell phones operate by connecting to indiscernible frequencies. Because we can't hear or see these frequencies, we take them for granted. Yet we rely on these receivers to pick up the frequencies and use them to deliver messages to us. In the same way, intuition is a frequency that is constant and available at all times.

Think of monkey mind chatter as static that interrupts the frequency wave of our intuition being picked up by our radio receiver. Our monkey mind not only plays havoc with our intuition, but also can affect how we receive personal oracles. This formidable opponent attempts to drag us, kicking and screaming, back into the limitations of three-dimensional reality, where the mind can remain in control. Controlling the monkey mind requires developing a new mental muscle that enables you to outmaneuver the chatter. You need to flex and stretch and build this muscle so that it has the strength to tame the monkey mind.

So how do we do this?

It helps me when I break the mind down into left-brain, right-brain functions. Mind chatter is left brain: logical, sequential, and focused on small details. The right brain is creative, intuitive, and comprehends the bigger picture. Dr. Jill Bolte Taylor, a Harvard-trained brain scientist, referred to the massive stroke in the left hemisphere of her brain as a blessing and a revelation. It taught her that by "stepping to the right of her left brain," her right-brain feelings of well-being that had been sidelined by left-brain "logic" were able to take center stage. Now, unable to use her left-brain logic, she was forced to rely on her senses, gut feelings, and hunches, and to expand her focus to encompass the larger picture.

When we learn to tame our monkey mind chatter, the wisdom of our right hemisphere can slip right past the disruptive chatter and sync with the left brain to validate the wisdom of our intuition. Clinton Hartmann, internationally known pioneer in the field of surface acoustical wave devices, describes his tried-and-true method for switching from left brain to right brain. He relies on this method when his logical, sequential left brain runs into a roadblock and can't reach the solution to a problem. That's when he switches to right-brain mode, which also works to disengage left-brain mind chatter. Here's his description of how it works.

Let's say I have some problem or question for which I want an answer. Concentrating harder and harder is not getting me to the answer; it's only making me uptight. I find that if

I can relinquish the intense process of trying to figure out the answer and accept the fact that deep thinking—a skill that is an important part of being me—is not working for this problem, I can clear my mind. Once that happens, I mentally envision moving the problem to the intuitive side of my brain, which will "know" the answer either immediately or in due course. I don't try to forget the problem. Instead, I give up the struggle and hand the problem to that part of me that does not deal with equations, logic, or words, but is the seat of a deeper appreciation for the underlying meaning of equations and other quantifying vehicles. This other side deals more with pictures, textures, color, beauty, symmetry (or beautiful asymmetry), and emotions. In my perception, the two sides of my mind primarily communicate with each other through mental pictures. Once the problem is handed from left brain to right brain, it helps for me to make drawings, find related pictures on the Internet, and either physically or mentally visit locations related to the problem. Inevitably, the answer will come to me.

So when you get an intuitive message and your mind starts to draw you off course, here are some steps you can take.

TIPS FOR TAMING MONKEY MIND CHATTER

1. Learn to recognize the monkey's voice and catch him chattering.
2. Do not dialogue with the chattering mind.

3. Instead, thank your rational mind for the brilliant job it does for you. Then invite your mind to relax and be still. You may even want to imagine yourself ushering your rational, logical left brain into a comfy chair!

4. Step to the right of your left brain.

5. Refocus your attention on your original intuitive hit and let it "speak" to you.

6. If the rational mind pops back in, switch off the chatter. Imagine adjusting your channel dial in your mind, eliminating the static, picking up the strong frequency.

7. Repeat this process as needed.

Keep in mind that taming monkey mind chatter is a process. Don't worry how many times you need to repeat these steps. Be gentle with yourself. It takes commitment, time, and patience to create new patterns of behavior. In a world that's filled with mysterious messages designed to resonate through your sixth sense, it's worth getting a rein on that monkey!

SHARPENING AND EXPANDING YOUR INTUITION

Just as it takes practice to quiet monkey mind chatter, it takes practice to fine-tune your intuition. It's like working out at the gym, or practicing the piano, or honing the craft of painting. The more you do it, the more you will recognize and rely on your intuition and the messages it delivers. Fortunately, sharpening intuition is not as mystical as you might think. It's as simple as tuning in to your favorite radio station and listening as it broadcasts personal oracles directly to you.

Once again think of yourself as a radio receiver. You can choose to tune in to AM, FM, or satellite stations. Standard reception on all receivers is AM. It's important to note the standard frequency is more susceptible to static (monkey mind chatter). FM reception offers a wider range of frequencies that are more complex and stronger. And satellite reception reaches an even broader band of frequencies. Some of us are quite content to live our lives within the limits of AM stations. Others are willing to invest in FM, while still others want every bell and whistle that's available to upgrade their reception to the broader band of satellite reception.

If you're interested in upgrading your reception, here are some how-tos delivered to me one day from my mentor Richard Deertrack. Kenneth and I were driving into Santa Fe for the day. I had been gazing aimlessly out the passenger window when something attracted my attention to an ancient Native American face in a cloud. My intuition told me to stay tuned in. I did just that and began to recognize the familiar energy of Deertrack, who had died three years earlier. Normally I would have grabbed my camera and snapped a photo, but my camera was at home. I used the opportunity to be totally present in the moment. As I looked into Deertrack's eyes, I could feel him looking back at me. I could feel the intensity of our well-established energy reconnecting and sensed an invisible cord of communication between us.

Then, just as he did in life, Deertrack began to teach me. I grabbed pen and paper and recorded his teachings.

© *The Taos News*

These are the exact words that Deertrack gave me to share with you.

What else does your personal oracle have to teach you?
Are there other messages or expansions of the message
you received?

Meditate on your personal oracle and learn what else
it has to teach you.

Everything expands, everything is larger than we
perceive. Expand each experience. Meditate; let the per-
sonal oracle talk to you. Let it explain itself and offer more
information. Meditate on each experience.

Then he offered some ideas on how to do this:

Write. Draw. Dream. Share. Allow yourself to go deep,
wide, high, inside, outside. Allow yourself to soar. . . .

Next Deertrack offered these three steps for how a personal oracle works:

Step 1. Spotting the personal oracle.

Step 2. Your interpretation.

Step 3. Allowing personal oracles to expand the message and teach you.

Notice the word "meditate." Deertrack has always used the word "meditate" to refer to a process—taking time to allow something to germinate naturally into fullness. He reminds us that our first impression of a personal oracle message is only the beginning, the first step, the face value, if you will, of what a message has to teach us. He encourages us not to stop there but to allow the personal oracle to continue to teach us.

His instruction to allow everything to expand is also what we're doing when we upgrade our sixth sense. We extend our capability to pick up other frequencies and dimensions that resonate in accordance with our ability to notice and receive them. Then, as the body of our experiences expands, our sense of being isolated and alone is replaced with an awareness of our secure place in an interconnected universe.

EXERCISES TO SHARPEN AND EXPAND YOUR INTUITION

Let's take a look at some easy and effective ways to heighten our awareness of the energies that exist all around us. Some work with us to quiet the mind. Others upgrade our receivers automatically, like loading the latest apps on our personal electronic devices. I'll also give you some exercises to help you connect more easily with other energy frequencies and dimensions. Choose those activities that resonate with you. It may be one activity; it may be all of them. If you're the bells-and-whistles type and eager for more apps, check out the appendix.

Creating a Sacred Space

My introduction to the ritual of creating sacred energetic space was born of necessity. I thought I *had* to work eight hours a day, seven days a week, to achieve my goal. I was logging a lot of unnecessary, unproductive hours. But this wasn't working for me. The voice of my intuition became muffled.

The game changer was this exercise.

- Select a specific chair.
- Remain in that chair for at least thirty minutes every day.
- While there, meditate, read, research, let your creative energy flow.

I tried it, and it didn't take long before I noticed my creative energy increasing. Instead of forcing myself to work, I looked forward to being in that specific chair at that particular desk. What was different? The energy had shifted. I was investing less time and accomplishing more. My own divinely inspired energy was building and holding space for me and welcoming me each time I returned.

My office/sacred space is now one of my favorite places to be in the world. The creative energy keeps on increasing. The energy of this space now has an accumulation of supportive energy that embraces me each time I return.

The possibilities are endless. Your ritual sacred space could be like Liza's Starbucks in Milwaukee, where she goes to write her latest novel. She sits in the same chair at the same table every time she visits. She says she can feel the energy shift and click in the moment she sits down.

You don't need to be working on a project to benefit from tuning in to the energy of your own sacred space. Some create their sacred energy space for healing and maintaining a sense of balance. My friend Annalisa instinctively created this kind of space with a red chair in her living room. She placed objects that held positive energy for her within arm's reach of her chair: a wish pillow, photos, and a few other personal things. When she was feeling down or lonely, she would sit in her red chair, cradle the pillow in her arms, and press it tightly against her heart. She felt recharged by this accumulation of positive energy. The red chair became her place of tranquillity, a place where she always felt a sense of comfort and peace. This palpable energy increased whenever she spent time there. It remained to welcome her like a warm, cozy blanket each time she returned. She told me that she never shared the significance of this chair or her ritual with her family, and by doing so was able to safeguard her sacred energy right in the middle of a family area!

If you want to experience this energy yourself, it's simple and easy to do. Just select a place that appeals to you, one that you can return to. Continue to go to that specific place over and over and over, and then pay attention to what you feel. Tune in to your intuition and sense your energy that has built up in the space.

Meditation

Your sacred space is ideal for meditating, and meditating is an ideal way to open access to and sharpen your intuition. If you don't have a sacred space, a couch, chair, or the floor will work just fine. In case you've never meditated, I've outlined the process below.

Don't worry about reading instructions and trying to do the exercises at the same time. There will be no pop quiz; no one will be checking to see if you're doing it the right way. Do it your way. Setting your intention sets everything in motion.

Meditation to Activate Your Intuition

Traditional meditation is used to quiet the analytical mind and create a state of receptivity and balance. As we learn to relax into this stillness, our hearts open and we reconnect with the essence of our being.

Choose a comfortable place to sit. Before you begin, take a deep breath. As you exhale, see yourself releasing the cares and concerns of your day. Now take a second deep breath. This time, as you exhale, see this breath carrying away anything that was hanging on. On your third and last deep breath, inhale deeply and, as you exhale this breath, bring yourself and all of your energy into this moment.

- Place your left hand on your forehead and your right hand on your belly. Your third eye is located in the center of your forehead. It functions as a gate that leads within to inner realms of higher consciousness and is considered the intuitive mind. Your belly is your solar plexus, your center of power and the rational, logical mind. By connecting these two areas you create an open state of receptivity and balance between them. This allows your intuition to speak more clearly to your rational mind.

· Inhale deeply and slowly from your diaphragm, then exhale slowly and fully.
· In your mind's eye, observe your breath flowing from your third eye to your belly and back again and again.
· As you breathe, notice the rhythm of your breath as it opens your third eye.
· Continue breathing this way until you feel like it's time to stop.

(Inspired by meditations of Yogi Bhajan, founder of 3HO Healthy Happy, Holy Organization)

Meditation to Integrate Left Brain and Right Brain

· Place your left hand on your throat and your right hand on your belly.
· Inhale deeply and slowly and then exhale fully and slowly.
· In your mind's eye, watch your breath flow easily from your throat to your belly and back again and again.
· As you breathe in and out, notice the rhythm of your breath connecting your abstract mind and your rational mind.

- Continue breathing this way until you feel like it's time
  to stop.

Cloud Gazing

As a kid, did you ever lie on the ground with your friends and
gaze up at the clouds floating across the arc of sky? My friends
and I would let our imaginations soar with those clouds as they
morphed into different shapes and images. Some shapes, like
pigs, ducks, snakes, boats, and bikes, were easy to identify, while
others remained obscure, cloaked in mystery. We never gave any
thought to how we were doing all of this; we were just playing. But
our intuition was automatically engaged each time a specific
image resonated with us.

Tips, tools, and ways to exercise and develop your psychic
muscles:

- Be still and bring yourself into the moment.
- Look softly into the clouds. What do you see?
- There is no rush; if there's a message, it will emerge.
- Let go and allow your attention to be tugged; then focus
  on the image that is tugging you.
- Tune in to your intuition a bit more and check to see if
  the image has a message for you.

This is where your right brain and left brain begin to dance
and your intuition makes some interesting personal connections
that incorporate thoughts and feelings.

For example, the pig might remind you of the expression
"When pigs fly," and suddenly you feel excited and empowered.

You feel like the universe is offering you a personal oracle. It is saying, *"Here's your flying pig—it is possible, now go for it!"* The boat might be a sign that validates your plans to make a journey of some sort. The bike might be a heads-up encouraging you to get back on the bike and do something you're afraid to do—or even to exercise.

There is no need to limit this activity to sunny, cloud-dappled days, when cloud images are clear and simple to define. A seasoned cloud gazer develops a special skill for tuning in to overcast or stormy skies. Gazing into a dark and threatening sky requires us to look more deeply in order to discern the images and messages that lie camouflaged within the varying shades of cloud cover. By using what's already familiar and comfortable, you can go deeper and expand your sixth sense and fine-tune your senses.

When interpreting cloud messages, be it a day of bright sunshine and blue sky or a day without a speck of blue peeking through the cloud cover, keep these points in mind:

- There are no incorrect interpretations.
- Clouds can mirror timely messages that come from our subconscious.
- Conduit clouds that link us with another dimension are accompanied by a unique sense of presence. For me, it's the sensation I get when someone is staring at me.

It can be fun and enlightening to play in the clouds. They are my go-to source when I'm scouting for personal oracles. Unless, of course, the sky is a clear blue without a cloud in sight, as it often is in my home state of Arizona. (In that case, turn on your computer and log onto www.oraclesinthesky.com and click on the

"What Do You See?" section. You'll find a virtual cloud playground right in front of you.)

One more thing about intuition to keep in mind as you continue to investigate your personal oracles and amass your own body of experiences. Intuition can do two things. One, it can guide a person to a personal oracle delivery system, and two, it can serve as the delivery system. The itchy feeling in the top of her head was the intuitive delivery system that perked up Karen's attention and kept the barefoot family safe from the bark scorpion that was crawling across the kitchen floor. An intuitive feeling draws my attention to personal oracles in clouds—like the protector cloud, and my father's cloud profile the day after he died.

Now that you have more tips and clues to help you investigate your world of personal oracles, I hope you're inspired to discover them for yourself.

Chapter 6

Personal Oracles as Healing Tools

How They Heal and Empower You

*It's easy to scoff at beliefs in the supernatural
when we don't understand their foundations.
Magic becomes apparent when the world cannot
be negotiated without its application. When we
do need to let ourselves believe, we do.*

—ALLAN HAMILTON, M.D.

In his book *The Scalpel and the Soul: Encounters with Surgery,
the Supernatural, and the Healing Power of Hope*, Dr. Allan
Hamilton, a Harvard-trained neurosurgeon, shares the following personal oracle story.

*Once, I was driving into the hospital to perform surgery
when I had to slam on the brakes suddenly because three
buzzards were standing in the middle of the road, shredding the carcass of a dead jackrabbit. When I got to the
hospital, as my patient was being wheeled into my*

operating room, I heard his wife lean over him, kiss him on the forehead, and refer to him as "my little bunny." I canceled the case. The warning of the buzzards was not a coincidence. Four hours later, the man suffered a massive heart attack. It probably would have been a fatal one, had it occurred in the middle of my surgery—if I hadn't heeded the warning from those buzzards! Having a myocardial infarction can become a terrible problem under anesthesia.

When Dr. Hamilton heard the wife call his patient "my little bunny," the image of the dead rabbit and the buzzards flashed back into his mind, and he slid the pieces of the supernatural puzzle into place. He recognized the rabbit as a sign, a message that he needed to heed. Fortunately for the patient and his family, Dr. Hamilton trusted his inner wisdom and had the courage to act on it.

He goes on to say: "As a practicing neurosurgeon, I found it maddening that no matter how assiduously I would hone my personal technical skills, or build my fund of knowledge, I could not overcome the influence the supernatural played every day in my operating room. For example, I learned to never hesitate to cancel a surgery if the patient felt unlucky on that day, or had a premonition of impending death."

Though he wasn't taught to do so in medical school, Dr. Hamilton learned to integrate conventional medicine with the Native American concept of spiritual medicine. He was able to see the supernatural just beneath the surface. As he writes: "It only took a small definite shift in my vantage point to see it."

According to Native American culture, the health of an individual is inextricably linked to the people and objects

surrounding that person. Native American healing practices create harmony between the physical environment and the world of
spirit. As Jamie Sams and David Carson write in *Medicine Cards:
The Discovery of Power Through the Ways of Animals*: "Spiritual
medicine is anything that improves our connection to the Universe and to all life, which includes the healing of body, mind and
spirit. This medicine is also anything that brings personal power,
strength and understanding."

By definition, personal oracles respond to a need. It stands to
reason, then, that they come out of the woodwork when it comes
to health issues. It's empowering when you don't have to rely on
an expert to tell you what may be wrong. Be confident and trust
your intuitive tugs. As you'll read in the following stories, lives
were saved by acting on that intuition. Some of these oracles were
spontaneous, some appeared in response to a request. You never
know where a personal health oracle will appear—TV, radio, a
rainbow, an animal, a book, a remedy falling into your hands, a
gut feeling, a synchronicity. Don't be afraid to ask the universe
for assistance. Keep your receiver on and listen when an intuitive
message seems to come to you out of the blue. It may just nudge
you onto an invisible moving sidewalk that refocuses your life in
a new direction.

Nina had been using homeopathic and herbal remedies for the
past fifteen years to treat acute illnesses like sore throats and
colds. For more serious conditions, she always consulted her
family doctor, a seasoned homeopath. Recently, he'd been treat-
ing Nina for those pesky hot flashes related to menopause. In fact,
she was waiting for him to return from an extended trip to Europe

so she could pick up some medicine from him. He tailored the remedies to each patient's symptoms and constitution. Nina was weary of the bursts of sweating that were hitting her day and night, and had toyed with taking herbs such as black cohosh and the Chinese herb dong quai, often recommended for menopausal symptoms, but decided to wait a bit longer for her doctor's tailor-made medicine that always seemed to work best.

Nina went to a store selling homeopathic remedies. The remedies were stored in three-inch-long narrow plastic tubes stacked in alphabetical columns. As she reached for a bottle of kali phos, she glanced down to recheck the list of remedies she needed, and a tube tumbled off the shelf. She caught it and read the label, *Lachesis mutus*, "for hot flashes associated with menopause." Nina could hardly believe it. Of course she bought it!

Back at home, she looked it up online in a Materia Medica guide that lists symptoms and homeopathic remedies. The remedy addressed Nina's symptoms, so she took the doses as recommended. By the next day, she noticed that her symptoms had eased. The duration between hot flashes, as well as their severity, had decreased. When she spoke to her doctor five days later, he said that yes, that remedy was appropriate and it was fine for her to use on a short-term basis.

Nina says she's still amazed by the universe's answer to her quandary and the specific assistance that was offered. Wouldn't you love it if the answer to your needs jumped right into your hands?

It's also encouraging when something you do is instantly validated. Kenneth and I were a couple of hours into an eight-hour road trip when my husband started squirming in his seat. Finally he asked, "Ann, do we have anything to ease back pain?" The only pain reliever we had on hand was Excedrin for sinus headaches. I wasn't sure if that would work for back pain, but an idea came to mind that I had never tried. "You could reprogram it with the intention to ease your back. Do you want to give it a try?" He rocked his aching back easily from side to side and finally said, "Why not? I guess it's worth a try."

I handed him the pill, and he swallowed it with a swig of water. Within minutes an NPR reporter on the radio started talking about a study that charted the positive effects of placebos. Researchers had studied three groups. Group number one was given the actual medication. Group number two was given a placebo, thinking it was the actual medication. And the third group knew that the pill they were taking was a placebo. All groups reported varying degrees of positive results—even the group that knew it was taking the placebo. The radio report seemed tailor-made for Kenneth. Its data was an empowering message for him. In addition, it arrived immediately after we started our own "placebo study": reprogramming a pill with intention. Talk about synchronicity!

Kenneth's back pain did go away. Did the substances in the Excedrin relieve his back pain? Maybe, but maybe not. The synchronistic timing of the report is what fascinated us. It seemed more like a validation of what we were doing than a coincidence. Don't you just love it when relevant information appears like magic to reassure you? I'll bet you have some stories of your own to share.

Medicine doesn't always come in the form of a pill. Sometimes it appears in the form of timely information delivered from places we least expect. Sherri was having a difficult time with her employer. He was being especially aggressive and demanding to the point that she started having chest pains. Then one day on a whim, she tuned in to a webcast of Oprah's show *Lifeclass*. The topic of discussion was how to deal with difficult people and the internal negative reaction they can cause. Sherri listened to the challenges other people faced when dealing with bosses, coworkers, friends, and family. The featured expert offered one coping tool after another. This was just the information Sherri needed. She applied those tools to her own life and it began to ease the hold her boss had on her emotions. Within weeks, her chest pains disappeared.

Healing also can be spontaneous. An intriguing case of a mysterious healing comes from a man in New Mexico. It all started when a squamous cell cancer appeared on his leg. He recognized it because it was similar to one he'd had surgically removed a few months earlier. That procedure was done under a local anesthetic in the doctor's office and had gone like clockwork. So when the man found the recurrence of cancer cells, he thought it would be no big deal to have removed. That is, until he found the original surgeon was unavailable and so he met with a new one.

The first alarm went off in his head when his new doctor insisted on scheduling the surgery as an outpatient procedure in the hospital. Something in his gut said, *This doesn't feel right.* It seemed like overkill, even before she started talking about using a general anesthetic and then went on and on about how general anesthesia can sometimes result in death. Another alarm sounded when she required a release from his heart doctor, which hadn't been required before. A voice inside his head called out, *What's going on? This was nothing like this the first time around.* A calming voice inside his head answered, *Don't worry, everything is going to be okay.*

As the date for the surgery approached, he tried to forget about the cautionary alarms and remember the voice that said everything would be fine. Yet his discomfort with the new doctor nagged at him. He had no doubt that the cancer needed to be removed; it was growing right before his eyes. The stiff little cone shape with a hook on top was about a quarter of an inch long. It was tender to the touch, so he started keeping a bandage over it. He was surprised when the last Band-Aid stayed in place for a week, through all of his sports activities and daily showers.

The Saturday before his scheduled Monday morning surgery he decided to take the tenacious Band-Aid off and remove the adhesive residue that was sure to be left behind. As he pulled off the Band-Aid he heard a faint *plink*. Something hit the floor. He checked the area on his leg where the squamous cells had been. His leg was perfectly smooth—no marks, no indentation at the spot where the growth had been. Nothing! He looked on the floor and there it was, lying on the tile right beside his toes.

Sometimes he wonders what triggered the spontaneous healing. Was trouble lurking in the scheduled surgery? Or did the universe have something else up its sleeve? He'll never know the answer. But one thing he does know for sure. He's grateful the universe responded to his need, and for those hidden hands that worked their magic.

⌣

Between horrible bouts of high fevers and chills, Rachel ached for her fifteen-month-old son and her husband. She had been admitted to the hospital three days before Thanksgiving to have her ileum, riddled by Crohn's disease, surgically removed, and now it was December 15, according to her tear-off calendar. Day and night had become indistinguishable; she was that sick and delirious, soaking her hospital gown with fevered sweat. Her release date had come and gone weeks ago. There was an abscess the size of a melon in her stomach. The radiologist had discovered it after six CAT scans, and continued to drain dangerous bacteria through a thin, flexible tube. A fistula had developed in her bowel. Despite numerous rounds of intravenous antibiotics, Rachel wasn't improving. The threat of death hovered close by. When awake, she had no energy to read or watch television. All she could do was lie there, often thinking about her husband and son and how they would fare if she didn't make it. She knew that the doctors didn't have a clue as to what else they could do to save her.

A knock at the door roused Rachel from her stupor. Expecting a nurse to walk in, she was surprised to see a man whom she had never met before. He introduced himself as a chaplain and asked if he might visit for a moment.

"How are you doing today?" he asked. His kind eyes and gentle manner relaxed Rachel.

"To be honest, not well. I'm . . . I'm afraid I might die. Even though the doctors haven't said they're worried, I see it on their faces."

"What faith are you, dear?" asked the chaplain.

Rachel said, "I'm Jewish."

"Would you mind if we prayed?" Rachel shook her head, indicating that would be fine. The chaplain moved his chair next to the bed. He took one of Rachel's hands in his rough, strong ones.

The moment the chaplain began praying out loud, warmth

flooded her body. It felt much stronger than the warmth from the chaplain's hands. Its current carried hope and assurance that all would be well. Rachel closed her eyes and allowed the feeling to take over her.

The chaplain finished. "I'll continue to pray for you." He squeezed her hand and left.

Immediately Rachel felt better, and she continued to improve. Within a few hours, she could sit up, and within a few more hours she was walking the ward hallway. Within a week, the abscess and fistula had shrunk and disappeared. The doctors were left in awe. Rachel understood what had happened. This healing had nothing to do with the doctors.

I especially like this story because the delivery system that responded to Rachel's need to be healed was a religious man of a different faith who helped her tap into the power of prayer. After all, personal oracles are ecumenical.

Healing personal oracles also translate through flashes of insight that occur like a download of knowing. They can alter our body-mind-spirit connection and facilitate healing on a deep level.

Dr. Christiane Northrup shares this empowering story in her book *Women's Bodies, Women's Wisdom.*

One of my patients told me, "I had a flash of insight on the way to your office today. When I was little, the only way I could get my mother's attention was to be sick. So I've had a lot of broken bones, then cancer, and now an abnormal Pap smear. I just realized today that I don't have to get sick to get her attention anymore!" She added that at the moment

she had that insight in the car, the sun broke through the
clouds, reinforcing her insight with its brilliance.

The solution to the following problem did not occur in a flash; it materialized gradually along an invisible moving sidewalk. Steven's disease didn't fit into a category. It was like multiple sclerosis, but it wasn't. It had overtones of ALS, but it wasn't. The doctors knew only that it was a degenerative disease of the muscles and nerves. When experimental treatments began causing more problems, Steven's wife, Taylor, decided to start investigating alternative therapies. This was in the early 1990s, when visits to the library still unearthed more information than an Internet search.

Taylor investigated Chinese medicine and acupuncture, looked into different modalities of energy healing, such as Reiki, searched for dietary information, and made appointments with practitioners. Nothing really seemed to be helping or even felt right.

Feeling at a dead end one day, Taylor stopped at a bookstore that catered to the metaphysical and holistic crowd. Perhaps she could find some answers there. Once inside, however, she didn't know which way to turn, so she stood amid the soothing smell of sandalwood incense and sent out a silent request to the universe to guide her because she was at a loss.

She began perusing books in the health section, pulling out a title here, a title there, and skimming the pages. Finally she settled on a book that tugged at her and felt right, even though she had never heard of the author or its subject matter. The book was *Perfect Health*, and was the fifth book by the then relatively unknown Deepak Chopra. It was his first book about Ayurveda, the eastern Indian science of daily living. Little did Taylor know that in the process of answering her request, the universe had nudged her onto an invisible moving sidewalk.

Taylor found the book intriguing. She happened to show it to a coworker, who said, "My brother is into Ayurveda. He lives in Fairfield, Iowa, and is part of the Maharishi Mahesh organization." That's where the Indian-born Dr. Chopra started his work in the United States. Taylor found her coworker's brother to be a great resource about the five-thousand-year-old system of Ayurveda.

The next person to help her in the journey was her hair-dresser. "Your husband should go see the new doctor in town from Denmark. He's really into holistic medicines." *What the heck is going on?* Taylor wondered. She booked an appointment for Steven.

In addition to having studied homeopathy and Chinese medicine, the doctor also had extensive training in Ayurveda. He offered an explanation of Steven's disease like no other medical professional they had consulted. Still driven by a need to learn as much as she could to help her husband, Taylor began attending the doctor's lectures on health and healing. When she learned that he was offering a seminar in Kathmandu, Nepal, called "Self-Healing in Ayurvedic and Tibetan Medicine," she felt a tug that could not be ignored. She and Steven ended up leaving their young children with relatives and traveling halfway around the world to attend.

The seminar had a huge impact on Taylor. It taught her much about healthy living and enabled her to make changes in her family's lifestyle. The kitchen became the medicine cabinet. The microwave went into retirement. A writer by profession, Taylor began penning articles about health and healing, and had articles and books published. Steven's condition improved, and he was able to live a full life.

Taylor's journey was one that she could never have imagined. She paid attention to the personal oracles that came her way—the intuitive tugs, books, articles, people—and with the assistance of the universe's guidance, allowed the journey to unfold.

This next story, about a dog called Floyd Henry, a boxer, gives new significance to the idea of dogs as man's best friend—or in this case, a woman's best friend.

Carol had always had a special spot in her heart for boxers, but when she rescued a seven-month-old boxer puppy, she never dreamed that years later he would save her life.

Carol was puzzled when Floyd Henry started gently nibbling her nose. This went on for a few days before she finally said, "What are you doing?" He placed his right paw on her right breast and pushed firmly. The dog repeated this a few times, always pushing purposefully in the exact same spot. Then he stood back and looked Carol right in her eyes. He seemed to be saying, "There's a problem here."

As an athlete, Carol had always tried to take good care of her body, which included having regular mammograms, but she'd just moved to a new town and hadn't found a new doctor yet. Thanks to Floyd Henry's persistent urging, she found one. The doctor diagnosed the problem as a benign cyst and chalked it up to Carol drinking too much coffee.

But Floyd Henry continued to act strangely. Every time Carol sat down, he sniffed at her nose. It reminded her of the story of a beagle in Florida that sniffed out cancer in his owner. After four days of sniffing, nudging, and pawing from her eight-year-old boxer, Carol made a second appointment. This time it was with the Winship Cancer Institute of Emory University.

When Carol was diagnosed with stage three breast cancer, she wasn't surprised to learn that the cancer was located in the exact spot where Floyd Henry had been placing his paw. According to oncologist Dr. Sheryl Gabram, Carol's cancer is hard to diagnose. "Her type of cancer presented as an indistinct asymmetric in her breast." She went on to say, "I absolutely believe the dog saved Miss Witcher's life."

Three years later Carol was cancer free!

After making her way through chemotherapy, surgery, and then radiation, she referred to her personal oracle journey as a "remarkable ride."

An interesting footnote: Part of Carol's remarkable ride was the study she participated in before she began treatment. It measured the types of gases exhaled by cancer and non-cancer patients. More than seventy percent of the time, the test accurately determined which patients had breast cancer and which ones did not. Studies such as this have been conducted in different parts of the world. The hope is that someday we will be able to walk into a doctor's office and breathe into a device that will diagnose with a high degree of accuracy whether or not we have cancer. In the meantime, keep your antenna up and be on the lookout for your own mysterious messages that can heal and empower you.

⌣

In an interview to promote his book *Anticancer: A New Way of Life*, David Servan-Schreiber, M.D., talked about the "stroke of luck" that saved his life. When a trial patient was a no-show,

Dr. Servan-Schreiber ran the brain scan on himself and discovered his own brain cancer, which would have gone undiagnosed until symptoms began to surface.

Was it a "stroke of luck"? Yes, but when viewed through the paradigm of personal oracles, we can see how the universe conspired in his favor, saving his life through the trial patient who didn't show up.

Forced to confront his own illness, Dr. Servan-Schreiber stepped onto his own invisible moving sidewalk that redirected his life. He was forced to confront what medicine knows about the illness, and all that's still unknown. He marshaled his will to live and then, inspired by a new and very personal purpose, set about understanding the body's natural cancer-fighting capabilities. In this fifteen-year journey, he went from disease and relapse into scientific exploration and finally to health. He now shares his findings with others.

Here is a well-earned sign of hope and healing for an ex-soldier with PTSD. Sixty-something Stan was shocked the first time he received a phone call from Snoopy, one of his Vietnam combat buddies whom he hadn't seen or talked to in more than four decades. The phone call was followed by photographs of seventeen-year-old Stan and his buddies in the jungle. As he showed them to Patricia, his wife of forty years, he pointed out the guys who were killed and his mood grew darker and darker. He seemed to retreat back into his cave after that.

Patricia had been receiving e-mails from Delta Company, Stan and Snoopy's unit, for quite a while before Snoopy's call. The e-mails detailed the particulars of their upcoming reunion in

2012. Each time one arrived, she showed it to Stan, but he wasn't interested. In fact, he wouldn't even discuss it.

"Let sleeping dogs lie," was all he said each time she mentioned going.

Patricia printed the information and tacked it up on her bulletin board behind her office door.

Then, on New Year's Eve 2011, Patricia received a call from their friend whose husband had been moved to a long-term-care facility. She was feeling lonely and looking for company. Stan encouraged his wife to go spend the night with their lonely friend, so she did.

Patricia arrived home around noon the next day so she and Stan could welcome in the new year together. Stan was sitting outside on the front porch in his rocking chair. She could tell when she walked up that he had retreated further into himself, and she wondered whether she should have stayed home with him. He said he had not had a very good night and was glad she hadn't been there. Snoopy had called, and he and Stan had reminisced about things that had happened to them when they were in Vietnam. Over the course of the evening, they dredged up some devastating memories that Stan had kept carefully buried all these years. He told Patricia they were still talking at midnight when the fireworks started. "Those fireworks kept going till dawn, and it was like being back in the war again." By the time he hung up the phone, he was feeling very low. Now Stan became quiet again, withdrawing to that place where he spent so much of his time now.

Patricia went inside and made a pot of coffee, then came out carrying a tray with two mugs of coffee and a plate of their favorite cookies. They sat quietly for a while before Stan started talking again. "Snoopy is sending a schedule for the Delta reunion in May. He wants me to go. He kept saying that we're brothers forever."

Patricia tried to find words to encourage him, to tell him that maybe it was best to let the bad things come and acknowledge them, but he was all tensed up and shaking his head. That's when she noticed a rainbow had settled on Stan's face.

"Stan! There's a rainbow! It's going right across your mouth and mustache!"

"I know. I can feel it." The strained look on his face softened. "It's warm. It feels so good, like sun rays." Stan pointed to the side of the house. "Hey, look, there's one on the wall here, too."

They didn't talk about the hope the rainbow symbolizes, or the fact that an extension of that rainbow had landed on their home, but they were both affected by the energy. Stan relaxed a bit and words came more easily for Patricia. She found herself saying some things that had been on her mind for a long time.

"Honor the memories, instead of just acknowledging them."

"Turn it into love."

Stan had relaxed a bit but was still stuck in the past. His response would remain the same, at least for a little while longer. "Oh no, I'm going to my grave with it."

Patricia wasn't just throwing out platitudes; she was speaking from personal experience. She'd already managed to turn her anger into love. For years and years she had picketed and protested any form of war the military was engaged in. Then at some point she realized that the energy of her anger was actually feeding and expanding the warring energy. That's when she changed her tactics. She stopped picketing and started showering the military establishment with love energy.

They finished their coffee and cookies. Patricia got her box of heart confetti from her office. She and Stan drove to the war surplus store to spread love like they had done so many times in the past. They parked in front of the large mural of soldiers holding the American flag, beside a military jeep that was always on the lawn. Stan sat in the car with the motor running; Patricia hopped out of their Tahoe and spread hearts at the foot of the mural, then dumped what remained of her stash of hearts into the jeep. Stan called out in a loud whisper, "Come on, come on, someone's going to catch you." When Patricia turned to get back in the Tahoe, a tiny white feather floated out of nowhere. Stan saw it, too. Patricia told me that tiny white feathers seem to appear at important moments in her life. They are a sign to her that an angel is around.

A couple of days later she showed Stan the information about the reunion. He had no memory of ever talking about it. She could almost see his armor of protection slide open a bit as he said, "Okay, let's plan to go."

Patricia said seeing the crack in Stan's armor felt like a climax to a life phase. Now a new chapter was opening. "Stan and I decided to make 2012 a theme year: 'Yellow Submarine.' There's a line in that Beatles song—'As we live a life of ease, every one of us has all we need.'"

For Stan and Patricia, the rainbow—a signal of hope for so many of us—was a precursor of a transformation that was about to occur. And the feather was further confirmation for Patricia that help was nearby.

WHERE OUR INTUITIONS ORIGINATE

Did you know that our gut feelings originate in the solar plexus?
Where is the solar plexus located? Place the palm of your hand on
your stomach just above your navel. This is your solar plexus. The
solar plexus is a major intuitive center, a barometer, if you will,
that lets us know whether we're safe or not. It can even signal to
us when we're being lied to.

I was fascinated to learn that the solar plexus is called "the
primitive brain," and that it actually operates independently from
the brain in our head. In his book *The Second Brain*, Columbia
University researcher Michael Gershon, M.D., details the discovery and gradual scientific acceptance of how the enteric (intesti-
nal) nervous system operates in this way. He describes the second
brain as our sensory brain. It consists of an extensive network of a
hundred million neurons, approximately the same number found
in the brain in our skull. Located in our intestines, it sends out
signals through physical sensations that are commonly referred
to as gut feelings. Like the brain in our skull, it is able to learn and
remember, but this brain produces emotion-based feelings.

You may already be familiar with the messages you receive
from the solar plexus. If not, take a few minutes and tune in to
your "second brain." Place one hand on your solar plexus and the
other hand on your heart, then be still. Tune in to your body. Does
your body have a message for you today?

As we consider some of the ways the universe interacts with
us to keep us healthy, let's take a look at those mysterious gut
feelings and intuitive hits that can prod us into action and even
save our lives, as one did for the man in the next story.

⌐

Maggie slid quietly out of bed before her husband, Patrick, awakened. She and her husband were early birds, but this day was particularly special. She was going to meet some girlfriends for their annual Christmas Eve breakfast at the Ski Shack. She was blow-drying her hair, thinking about the piping hot coffee and decadent warm cinnamon rolls they served at the Ski Shack, when she noticed Patrick still lying in bed with the covers pulled up to his chin.

"Hey, sleepyhead, I thought you were hitting the slopes early," she said.

Patrick mumbled something about wanting to sleep in. She couldn't remember the last time he had slept in, but he had been hitting the slopes pretty hard the past few days, and she knew from personal experience that it could tire you out. As she walked out of the bedroom, she blew him a kiss. He reached out from under the covers and caught it.

The coffee, rolls, and girl talk lived up to her expectations. After breakfast they always prowled through the shops in case there were any last-minute gift ideas they had missed. This year, for some reason, Maggie didn't feel in the mood to shop, so she headed home.

She expected her husband to be off with his buddies. When she drove up, he was just leaving to take the dogs for a walk. She watched him take a few steps and then stop. He leaned over and put his hands on his knees. She walked over to him. "Hey, honey, what's up?"

"Wow, I just don't have any energy. Something's wrong. My chest feels like something's sitting on it."

Maggie laid her hand on his back. "How about we have you checked out at the hospital?"

He agreed, but said he needed to stop in the bathroom first. While there, he took a couple of aspirins just in case. As they drove down the mountain to a lower altitude, the pressure in his chest started to ease. "We'll probably get to the hospital and it'll be like taking a car to the repair shop," he said. "They'll start checking me out and nothing will be acting up."

That wasn't the case. "Good thing you didn't play the macho card," the emergency room doctor said, "or you wouldn't have made it." Patrick had ninety-eight percent blockage in his main artery. A stent gave him a new lease on life, and he returned to living the athletic life he loved. And Maggie was grateful something had made her return home that day instead of shopping with her friends.

Several years later, Patrick listened to his intuition and dodged another bullet. This time no traditional symptoms warned him of impending trouble. Being an athlete, he was very in tune with his body. As he says, "Something just didn't feel right." He couldn't put his finger on exactly what it was. "My body was sending me a message I wasn't going to ignore."

He went in for an EKG, then met with his heart specialist, who looked at the results and said everything looked normal. They talked about the possibility that the EKG had failed to pick up something. The doctor offered to get him in for an angiogram first thing in the morning. "If something's going on, I can fix it right there, and if not, we'll know you're okay."

Maggie heard the term "widow-maker" for the first time when the doctor came out of the surgery to talk with her. The first thing he said was he wished all of his patients tuned in to their bodies as well as Patrick did. "He dodged the widow-maker again," said the doctor. "The area just outside the stent was acting up. Patrick had ninety-five percent blockage in his main artery, but we put in a new stent. Your husband is good to go!"

Three years after that blind date when Kenneth *mysteriously* rubbed the cramp in my neck and signaled our deep connection, we tied the knot and moved to southern California. We knew we were lucky to have found each other and anticipated a long future together. Not long after we settled in, however, I started having an empty sensation in my solar plexus. It was a sensation of dread. This uneasy feeling had a voice. I recognized it as the voice of my inner wisdom. This thought-voice was telling me, *"Get a mammogram—NOW!"*

In the days it took me to locate the mammogram center nearby and set up the appointment, the unrelenting sense of urgency grew stronger.

"NOW . . . NOW."

It wouldn't leave me alone, and thankfully so. An early mammogram identified "minuscule" cancer growing in my right breast. A lumpectomy removed the cancer before it had time to grow or spread, then the area was radiated to make sure the cancer was gone. If I'd ignored that gut feeling to get a mammogram, there's a good chance you wouldn't be reading these words.

When a gut feeling urges you to take care of yourself, pay attention. Determine what your inner wisdom is telling you and then muster up your courage and act on it. It could save your life!

Remember that you are never alone; you have the power of the universe on your side. Welcome that energy into your life and be on the lookout for those miracles that show up to help you co-create your health and well-being.

PART III

Life-Altering
Personal
Oracles and
Amazing Stories

Chapter 7

Crinkles in Time
Dreams and Visions

*I've learned that the limits of time and space are a
conspiracy of the mind. It is possible to go beyond
those things.*

—RAM DASS

Ah, the mystery and magic of dreams and visions. Whether
they visit during sleep or waking reveries or meditations,
dreams have never ceased to fascinate humans. As you
know from your own experience, dreams appear in all shapes,
colors, and degrees of clarity. Prophetic dreams prepare and
guide us. Other dreams illuminate dilemmas, help us cope with
loss and grief, and even diagnose illness. Still others offer clues to
scientific puzzles and inspire literature, art, and music, like Paul
McCartney's song "Yesterday," which came to him in a dream.
When he awoke, he attributed the melody he had dreamed to a
vague memory of some tune he heard during childhood. As it
turned out, the melody was original. He added lyrics, and "Yesterday" went on to become one of the most well-known pop songs

in the world. But in whatever form they appear and whatever message they convey, dreams and wide-awake visions are personal oracles that come along to guide and support us.

I like to call dreams and visions that occur outside linear time "crinkles in time." They occur when linear time—one dimension—steps aside for a moment to show us what might be coming our way in the future. In that moment, when the future steps into the present, we are allowed to glimpse a probability that is waiting to be activated in the quantum universe.

It helps when we consider these crinkles in time through the paradigm of quantum physics. In our quantum universe, some events are fluid possibilities of what is to come. They are not set in stone. Sometimes we are in a position to affect the outcome when given advance warning. You might think of them as ghost probabilities. Other prophetic dreams and visions, like a vision of a tsunami, leave us wondering if there was something we could have done besides pray for the best possible outcome.

CRINKLES IN TIME AND VISIONS

Let's start with this crinkle in time from the July 1, 2000, issue of *Psychology Today*.

Alex was cleaning his double-action six-shot revolver in preparation for a hunting trip later in the month. Before he started cleaning the gun, he removed the five bullets in the chamber. (He always left one chamber empty for safety reasons.) After he finished cleaning, he started reinserting the bullets into the cylinder. Nothing was out of the ordinary until he came to the fifth and final bullet. That's when he began to feel a strong sense of dread. It had something to do with that last bullet.

He was unnerved. Nothing like this had ever happened to him before. Something told him to trust his gut, so he put that bullet aside and decided as an extra precaution to leave the fifth chamber empty.

Two weeks later, when Alex, his fiancée, and her parents were staying at a hunting lodge, a violent argument broke out between her parents. Alex tried to calm them down, but in a wild rage the father grabbed Alex's gun from a drawer and pointed it at his wife.

Alex tried to intervene by jumping between the gun and the woman, but he was too late—he watched as the father pulled the trigger. For a horrifying split second, Alex knew that he was about to get shot at point-blank range. But instead the pistol went *click*. The chamber was empty. It was the very chamber that would have contained the fifth bullet—the bullet Alex had set aside two weeks earlier.

An account of the following crinkle in time was published in *The Huffington Post* on April 25, 2012. When I contacted Lynn Mesrobian-Darmon, she told me that she had been tuned in to messages from spirit since she was a child. But acting on one particular vision saved her daughter Ali's life.

Lynn refused to leave the hospital until doctors could tell her what was wrong with her fourteen-day-old daughter, Ali. "I knew something was wrong from the time I was in my third trimester," Lynn remembered. "But the doctor told me time and time again that everything was fine. And Ali did appear to be fine when she was born. But I knew even then that something was wrong. And the sense kept getting stronger."

Ten days after she brought her newborn home, while nursing her, Lynn glanced up at the bedroom mirror. In the reflection, she saw a gauzy white sheet over Ali's head. "I could just feel it was a warning," Lynn said. "It was what I'd been dreading. I knew we had to take her to the doctor. He said she was perfectly healthy and sent us home. But two days later, Ali was spitting up. So I took her to a hospital that specialized in children's care. Again, they said she was fine. I remember my then husband asking me if I felt better after that. I said to him, 'What we're going to go through hasn't even begun yet.' He just shook his head in disbelief."

Two days later, at another hospital, Lynn had to insist once more that her daughter was ill. Yet now doctors were worried more about Lynn than Ali. They thought she might be having a postpartum psychotic breakdown. Lynn, who as a mental health associate in a psychiatric unit had worked with women who had postpartum depression, knew there was nothing wrong with her. But in order to get help for her daughter, she agreed to be examined.

Before that happened, however, a pediatric infectious disease specialist examined Ali. He asked Lynn to explain what she thought was wrong. This doctor listened with real concern. He gazed deeply into the mother's eyes and *believed her when she told him that she felt that the problem was in Ali's abdomen.*

Although it was after five in the afternoon and the radiologists had left, the doctor ordered a CT scan and discovered that a toxic fluid was building up in Ali's abdomen. She had peritonitis—a fatal condition if it's not caught in time. Immediately the baby was in surgery. When nurses told Lynn that things looked serious, that she should call her family, she did so—even though, she recalled, she was sure then that her daughter was going to be fine.

Lynn was right. Ali has grown into a healthy young woman, and Lynn's ability to see into the future has become even stronger. Lynn now uses her psychic ability to help others.

PROPHETIC DREAMS

In the wake of disasters, multiple reports of prophetic dreams and oracles often surface. Immediately after the *Titanic* sank, dozens of people reported canceling their trip because of dreams that foretold of the sinking. It makes you wonder how many others had a similar warning but ignored it and paid the price. One businessman reported having a dream that warned him not to sail on the ship. This same dream repeated itself three times, yet he still chose to ignore the warnings. He was determined to make the trip, until something came up with his business that forced him to cancel.

⌐

A mother, a father, and their five children were all fast asleep when frantic screams jarred the parents wide awake. "Daddy's dead, Daddy's dead, Daddy's dead!" The parents rushed down the hall to comfort their hysterical son. The father picked up the four-year-old and held him close, patting him and whispering, "Everything's okay. Daddy's right here." Unable to calm the child, the parents brought him to their bed and tucked him safely between them, and the three spent a long and restless night nestled together. In the morning the boy was still upset. As they went through the familiar routine of getting all of the children fed and ready for the day, the parents realized they couldn't just drop the little guy off at day care as usual. They decided to alter their routine. The mother would take the older children to school, and the father would take their son to day care. The father phoned his office to let people know he'd be late for a scheduled meeting and then drove his son to preschool.

The father and son met with the boy's teacher to discuss what had occurred the night before. After making sure that the boy was calm and settled in his normal routine, the father clicked back into work mode and set off, late for his meeting at the Twin Towers in New York City. On the way, he checked for voice messages. There was one. He expected it to be an update about his nine o'clock meeting. Instead he heard his wife's frantic voice pleading, "Don't go into the city. Please don't. And tell me you're not there. Please, tell me you're not there. Turn around and come back home." A sick feeling overcame him. Something felt terribly wrong. She was practically crying. Then he heard her say, "An airplane just exploded into the Twin Towers."

The date was September 11, 2001. Thanks to their son's prophetic dream and their decision to prioritize their son's needs, the father never made it to his meeting, but drove back to their home in New Jersey unharmed.

By taking action on her prophetic dream, this woman kept her property safe. Sheila says that it was one of those dreams that you watch from outside the dream box; you're not in the cast of characters. The dream took place on some property Sheila owns in another state. A trailer sits on the property. In her dream, the trailer door was wide open, and all of the neighbors were milling in and out at random, throwing beer cans and trash all around.

The dream was unsettling. Sheila hadn't visited the property for some time since it was an eight-hour drive each way, but the message of the dream kept nagging at her. She decided to make a road trip to check on her property. Sure enough, when she arrived, the door was wide open and her trailer was trashed. Thanks to the dream, she was able to secure the trailer and avoid further problems.

This personal oracle was sent to me by my friend Ruth and appears as it was recorded in her dream journal.

In my dream I saw a car rolling and heard the crash. I knew my daughter was in the car. This dream repeated itself for several nights. Each time I put a big black X in the dream and said, NO! I'd never had such a dream before and felt quite disturbed by it. The next time I had the dream, I listened more carefully. Along with the crash sounds, I heard an unfamiliar, authoritative voice say, "She is going to be all right."

Ruth told me that a few days after having the dream with the voice, she received a call from the woman her grown daughter Lynne was visiting some fifteen hundred miles away. The woman was calling from the emergency room of a hospital. She informed Ruth that Lynne had been in a car accident and flipped her car three times. When the paramedics arrived on the scene and saw the condition of the car, they expected the passengers to be dead. Miraculously, Lynne suffered only a mild concussion and a broken toe. Thanks to the voice-message in her recurring dream, Ruth remained calm when she received the call. As she said, "I knew my daughter would be all right."

I asked Ruth what the X in the dream meant. Years ago, a psychologist suggested she visualize a big X over events and energies she wanted to block from entering her psyche. She's used it as a tool for years to dissipate negative images and fears that come her way. For her it works like a branding iron: when stamped on a scene or image, it dissipates the negative energy, and all fears fade away. Ruth never uses this method to deny what is occurring. She says it is a tool to block energy, like raising a fence to keep unwanted energy out.

Perhaps you've had your own prophetic dreams. I'll always remember one I had when my daughter Julie was about three. In the dream I walk to the edge of a swimming pool and look down into the water. There, at the bottom of the pool, is Julie's lifeless body clad in her pink-and-white-checked swimsuit. I awoke filled with dread, and from that moment on, I never could relax when Julie and I were around a swimming pool. I heaved a sigh of relief when she grew out of that little pink swimsuit and then dismissed the dream as irrelevant. I never gave any more thought to the idea of this dream being prophetic until I was working on this chapter. Then I realized that the image of Julie's dead body at the bottom of a swimming pool made me watch her even closer. Of course, I will never know for sure, but I'm beginning to wonder if the dream was a crinkle in time, giving me advance warning of a possibility that was out there. If that is true, perhaps the dream and the caution it generated in me saved Julie's life.

Have you ever had what seemed to be a prophetic dream and later dismissed it as irrelevant because you adjusted your behavior accordingly?

DREAMS OF SCIENTIFIC PROPORTION

Some of the greatest advances in scientific fields, from chemistry and biology to physics and engineering, were inspired by dreams.

German chemist Friedrich Kekulé had been working for many years to determine the molecular structure of benzene. One day while dozing in front of a fireplace, he dreamed of a snake seizing its own tail, thus forming a circle. When he awoke, he realized that the structure of benzene was a closed carbon ring. His dream image of the snake proved to be the missing link he needed to conceptualize the six-carbon benzene ring. With this model in place, other pieces of the organic chemistry puzzle fell into place. His discovery revolutionized modern chemistry.

Kekulé's contributions didn't stop there. He contributed valuable research on mercury compounds, unsaturated acids, and thio acids, and wrote a four-volume textbook.

During the German Chemical Society's elaborate celebration honoring the twenty-fifth anniversary of Kekulé's published paper on the benzene model, Kekulé concluded his remarks by saying, "Let us dream, gentlemen, and then perhaps we may find the truth."

⌣

Ever since James Watson and Francis Crick announced the structure of DNA in 1953, the genetic molecule has been making headlines. We may even take for granted the way scientists and doctors can now peek into our DNA to help diagnose our propensity to certain diseases. But did you know that their work was helped along by James Watson's dream? Some reports say that Watson conceptualized the double-helix structure of DNA after dreaming about a spiral staircase. The spiral staircase mirrored for him the shape taken by a DNA molecule. A helix is a three-dimensional spiral, like the shape of a spring or the railing of a spiral staircase. A DNA molecule consists of two helixes intertwined, and looks like a spiral staircase. Other accounts credit this breakthrough to a dream he had of two snakes intertwining. It's hard to know whether it was snakes or stairs. What we do know is that the inspiration appeared in a dream. Watson and Crick went on to win the Nobel Prize for their groundbreaking work.

⌣

Kudos to Albert Einstein and his dream that led him to formulate $E = MC^2$, the Theory of Relativity. Einstein said his entire career was an extended meditation on a dream he had as a teenager. He dreamed that he was riding a sled down a steep, snowy slope, and as he approached the speed of light in his dream, the colors all blended into one. Inspired by that dream, he spent much of his career thinking about what happens at the speed of light.

⌣

Have you heard the one about the cannibals and the sewing machine? That sounds like the first line of a joke, but it's not. It's how Elias Howe received the inspiration to design a machine with a needle that would pierce cloth. He had been struggling with the design when he had a dream that cannibals had captured him and were dancing around a fire, pumping their spears in the air in their ritual before cooking their prey. Howe noticed a small hole at the narrow tip of each spear. When he awoke, the image of that hole and the up-and-down motion of the spears remained with him. The idea of passing a thread through a needle at its narrowest point rather than at the wider end had not occurred to Howe before the dream.

Don't you just love dream messages, and the idea of being calm enough to notice a hole in the tip of each spear when you are about to become somebody's snack?

⌣

When Canadian Nobel Prize winner Dr. Frederick Banting was a boy, he could only stand by and watch as diabetes took the life of a fourteen-year-old friend, Jane. Losing his friend in such a traumatic way planted a seed in Banting to attend medical school. After practicing for a short time, he felt a calling to conduct research on diabetes, a disease that had continued to hold his attention. He believed that a part of the pancreas produced a substance that could treat the illness, though after creating piles of research, he still couldn't find the substance.

He'd had an especially exhausting day the night he fell asleep and was instructed in a dream to extract the degenerated pancreatic duct from dogs and study them. The dream provided the missing link. Banting extracted a substance from the pancreas of dogs that he called "isletin" and was later renamed "insulin." The first recipient was a fourteen-year-old boy who showed immediate improvement. Banting went on to win the Nobel Prize in Medicine at the young age of thirty-two. The passion ignited by the loss of a friend and inspired by a dream now stabilizes the lives of millions of diabetics around the world.

DREAMS OF ILLNESS

History is filled with accounts of dreams and dreamers who understood the value of utilizing messages delivered via dreams as clues and insight to healing. The ancient Greeks, for instance, relied on dreams to help predict and diagnose disease. Galen, who practiced medicine around A.D. 150, even wrote a treatise titled *On Diagnosis from Dreams.* Galen believed that dreams offered vital clues that could help healers diagnose and treat patients. Not only did he encourage people to carefully observe their dreams for clues to healing, but he was so confident in the information gleaned from dreams that he performed operations based on dream interpretations! Talk about patient-doctor cooperation!

⌐

The following prophetic dream gave this woman permission to do what so many of us wish we could do—take a time-out from our to-do lists.

> *I was going through a very long period of extreme stress when I dreamed that I was at a Renaissance fair. In the dream, I felt exhausted. I was riding a magnificent horse, but the horse kept getting smaller and smaller until it was the size of a pony, then a dog, and finally as small as a hummingbird. That's when it flew away.*
>
> *A year later I hit burnout for real while attending, of all things, a Renaissance fair. I was so exhausted I could barely get around. Then I remembered the warning about my diminishing energy as symbolized by the shrinking horse in the dream. I acknowledged my need for healing and arranged a major time-out from the main stressors in my life.*

So many times we forget our dreams the following day and never give them another thought until something comes along to jog our memory. That's when dream journaling comes in handy. Writing the dream down is the first step in the process. Seasoned dream journalers keep paper and pen beside the bed to record significant dreams, or pieces of their dreams, when they awake. Some skip lines and leave plenty of space between each dream so they can expand on the meaning of the dream or write them down when more pieces of the dream puzzle emerge from their memory.

Here's a tip for remembering a dream that is hazy when you wake up. Close your eyes and let yourself drift back into that relaxed state between dreaming and waking. Then invite your dream to return and replay its message.

Pam's fever had vacillated between 100 and 102 for about three days, and she had no energy to get out of bed. Aside from a slight cough, she had no other symptoms. Since none of the symptoms were that severe, she chose to sleep and let her body heal, rather than haul herself to the doctor's office.

On the fourth day of being sick Pam dreamed that she was walking on the softest, whitest material she had ever stepped on. It was dense but light, yielded to her weight but felt springy. The space she started out in appeared wide. As she traversed farther, heading downhill into a narrower space, she noticed that her feet began to sink deeper into the whiteness, which seemed to be turning gray. The material became soggier and soggier.

Upon wakening, Pam intuitively knew she had dreamed about her lungs. Could they possibly be filling with fluid? Even though she didn't feel any better or worse than the previous day, she asked a friend to drive her to the emergency room. Tests determined that Pam had a mild case of valley fever. Because the fever was in the early stages, she was sent home with this prescription: "The best medicine is to rest and you will be fine." Pam left feeling grateful that her dream had alerted her to the problem early and she avoided some potentially serious consequences. Indeed, within a week she had returned to work and most of her normal routine.

DREAMS THAT SOLVE PERSONAL DILEMMAS

Remember how Gandhi followed the guidance of a personal oracle that came to him in a dream? It inspired a strategy that helped India gain its freedom from Britain. Here are other oracle messages that have come through the conduit of dreams and offered a solution to a nagging problem.

Most golfers would love for a dream to fix their golf swing, as one did for the legendary golfer Jack Nicklaus. In 1964 he seemed to have lost his edge and was shooting scores in the high seventies. Then all of a sudden, his prowess returned. Nicklaus shares what happened:

> *Wednesday night I had a dream and it was about my golf swing. I was hitting pretty good in the dream, and all at once I realized I wasn't holding the club the way I've actually been holding it lately. I've been having trouble collapsing my right arm, taking the club head away from the ball, but I was doing it perfectly in my sleep. So when I came to the course yesterday morning, I tried it the way I did in my dream and it worked. I shot a sixty-eight yesterday and a sixty-five today.*

To this day, Nicklaus maintains the same technique.

⌒

Who hasn't had a dream that seemed important but its message was unclear? That's when a dream like Marsha's rerun dream comes in handy. Here's how she described the dream sequences that helped her grapple with a difficult family situation.

I had just returned home after spending the night at the hospital with my mother. Her surgery had gone on for hours, and the skilled surgeon told me that along with the ovaries, a piece of colon, and the spleen, he had removed a full gallon of cancerous fluid. He gave me a straightforward reply to my question "How long?" "Perhaps a year and a half," he said.

I fell asleep asking for guidance on how I should be approaching my life. How could I handle all the grief I was feeling? How could I have the energy to continue to work full-time and care for both my parents? How could I best give the love and support to my mother during her remaining time on Earth?

My dream was like a documentary presented in scenes. It starred three creatures: a rabbit, a tiger, and an eagle. In a strong, clear voice, an off-camera narrator explained three scenarios that responded to my requests for guidance.

1. *You must spend and conserve energy. Go about your chores like this rabbit, doing what must be done, then escaping into a burrow to rest as needed.*
2. *Like a tiger patiently watching and springing into action when the time is right, be aware. Look for opportunities to move forward. Notice everything, and be alert for*

dangers. Know when to be still and wait, when to move forward with swiftness and skill.

3. *Be able to move above in your perspective, like an eagle soaring on high above the big picture. Let the unnecessary fall away. Feel strengthened by the wind, the sun, the beauty around you. Be independent and strong.*

When the dream was over, a different voice said, "Run it again. She needs to see it again." Then it was as if someone pushed a replay button. The exact dream replayed. The same scenes of the three creatures played, and even the same words were spoken.

As soon as I woke up, I wrote down the dream. I had asked for guidance during a time of great pain and self-doubt, and I received it!

Marsha says that in the fifteen years since her mother passed, she's been strengthened by this advice many times. She keeps small statues of a rabbit, a tiger, and an eagle in her sacred space to remind her of the qualities she is working to cultivate in herself.

This sign of hope comes directly from another woman's dream journal. Her marriage of twenty-six years had disintegrated and a new life was beginning. She felt alone and feared for her future. This significant dream helped her view her life change more positively.

In the dream I am climbing up and then along scaffolding, feeling very frightened, unsure of myself. A large figure approaches me, but I can't distinguish its features. I know I can't back down, so I proceed slowly toward the figure. As it comes closer, I see that it is a construction worker in a hard hat carrying something. My fear transforms into curiosity as he hands me a small peat pot of dirt containing a green seedling. Although it's uncertain what the tiny plant will grow into, it is clearly thriving. He says something to me about nurturing it carefully.

When I interpret this dream, I'm reassured by the metaphors:

- *the scaffolding (all has collapsed around me and a new foundation is being built)*
- *the approaching figure (fear of the unknown)*
- *the tiny plant (my new life)*

Aspiring author Patricia Steele shares a dream that not only answered her question but inspired a lush setting for her novel.

Before I fell asleep I asked for some guideposts in my writing. Am I really a writer? Will I ever be published? I dreamed I was in this beautiful garden and there was a tree as big as a building, with steps winding all around it. Huge green leaves and fountains of water sprouted from its trunk. I climbed the steps and came to a desk with an old-fashioned typewriter on it. I was told that this was my office. It looked out over a thriving, verdant garden.

Patricia woke up feeling supported, with renewed hope that her novel would soon be completed and published. That day, she began incorporating the dream into her writing. As it turned out, the novel did get published. The story includes a tree in the back-yard of a restaurant named Café Wicked Peach Stone. Instead of steps going up the trunk, they lead down into the roots. That's where animals go when they die. They rest there, and they await reincarnation.

Lisa Hopper's path from successful medical professional to founder of a fledgling humanitarian aid organization was altered by a series of very specific recurring dreams. In her book *In the Wake of a Dream*, she shares how it happened.

Lisa sank into bed around midnight and drifted off to sleep. Sometime before dawn, while in the wake of a vivid dream, the sound of a horn honking in her neighborhood startled her awake. She tried to fall back to sleep, but the lingering images of the dream consumed her. The images were incredibly clear, but its meaning was not.

I am dressed in shorts and a T-shirt, standing in front of an airplane in the desert. The haze is just burning off in the morning sun, and I see the outline of mountains along the horizon. The airplane has "World Care" written on its side. I'm holding a clipboard and checking what seems to be a large load of shipping boxes spread out before me on the sandy airstrip.

She turned on her bedside light and recorded the lucid image with a picture in her journal. Then she flipped back the pages to read over other prophetic dreams, paying special attention to her notes on how the events they predicted came to fruition. Prophetic dreams weren't that unusual for Lisa. In fact, they had become an integral part of her life. She didn't talk about them much because she was afraid of being stigmatized by people thinking she was psychic. But something about the latest one intrigued her and sent her to her colleague Dellie, a psychologist with a special interest in dream interpretations and the teachings of Carl Jung. She told Dellie about her dreams and how some of them came true at later points in her life. "Your dreams are healthy," Dellie reassured her. "They're telling you something." She suggested Lisa visit a dream consultant she knew. Dellie even offered to go along.

A mystical-looking woman with long white hair and crystal-blue eyes greeted Lisa and Dellie at the door. The woman looked like a vision, dressed in purple, with a pink robe. She led them upstairs to a room where she conducted her sessions. When Lisa gave a fake name, the woman told her it wasn't necessary to give her a name at all.

The mystical woman told Lisa her energy was strong, but that she was resisting what was going on around her. She saw a lot of travel in her future. When she suggested that Lisa was a teacher, Lisa had a strong internal reaction. She had no interest at all in being a teacher and began to wonder if the woman was reading someone else—or making it up. Then she ended the session abruptly, saying, "This is all I will tell you. You have the gift. You will be given more information when you need it." She handed Lisa back her money and told her not to waste it consulting more people like herself. "Your path is already set and you will do great things," the woman said. Little did Lisa know the woman's insights would actually come true.

Soon afterward, Lisa ventured to Puerto Vallarta, Mexico, with a friend, and they stayed at a luxurious hotel. One warm afternoon Lisa felt the urge to roam around and soak in the *real* town off the beaten track. Within a couple of blocks of the hotel, the women stepped out of the world of haves into the world of have-nots. It was an environment overflowing with a desperate need that tugged at Lisa's heartstrings. There were hundreds of makeshift shacks pieced together from pallets and crates with no electricity or running water. One image stuck in her mind: a woman sitting beside her child, who was wrapped in a blanket and sleeping peacefully inside a cardboard box.

When Lisa returned from her holiday, she discovered that the hospital had been sold and her position would soon be eliminated. She began looking for new work. A series of fascinating jobs followed that involved travel, just like the mystical-looking woman had predicted. Everywhere she went, she ran into more desperate situations. She felt duty-bound to help those in need, and she always did whatever she could. But everything she was doing to help was short-term. She started to feel compelled to make a lasting change.

While working in Guatemala, the dream with the airplane recurred. Lisa went back to the States and began collecting school supplies to send to children in Guatemala and started setting up a humanitarian organization. When she shared what she was doing with friends, they wanted to become involved. Lisa needed a name for her burgeoning nonprofit business. Someone said, "Why don't you call it World Care, like in your dream?"

A series of other dreams clarified what Lisa was supposed to do. She realized that her dreams were all clues, pointing her in the right direction. Lisa was being given the personal oracle messages as she needed them.

Thanks to Lisa's recurring dreams and her unfailing commitment to making a lasting difference in the world, World Care Emergency Relief Center had collected and distributed more than 15 million pounds of resources valued at over $40 million in aid to humanitarian efforts worldwide by 2010. Whether they be victims of tsunamis, hurricanes, earthquakes, or tornadoes, or individuals in underdeveloped countries, World Care reaches out with resources and hope to those in need.

DREAMS WITH MESSAGES FROM BEYOND THE VEIL

When we lay our mind to rest and drift off to the land of dreams, we never know what wonders await us. Sometimes loved ones who've passed beyond the veil can visit us again, or send messages to let us know they are on their way. Some dreams deliver messages via an ancestor we never met.

After taking Rusty up on his offer to return in the form of another dog, I was following a series of mysterious cloud images and clues that seemed to be leading us closer to him. A breeder in Tucson, Auntie Maggie, had even agreed to call me when a litter of puppies was born so I could check them out. About a month or so before the litter was scheduled to arrive, I had a puzzling dream.

In my dream, Rusty was born, not in the litter I was waiting to check out, but to the "wrong mother." I woke up with a start and then nudged my husband awake to tell him about the dream. "What do you think it means?" I said. He mumbled something about not knowing and drifted back to sleep. I was lying there wide awake when I started having an incredibly strong sensation that Rusty was standing patiently at our front door. Later the same day, when I pulled in to Manor Care Assisted Living to visit my father, I noticed two clouds hovering directly above his wing of the building. They were shaped like those angels we see at Christmas, stretched out on their stomachs, blowing trumpets to herald the joy of the season.

Over dinner that evening, Kenneth and I were discussing the dream and that strange sense I had of Rusty standing at the front door when the phone rang. It was Auntie Maggie. "I just wanted to let you know that a different dog, one that I didn't know was pregnant when we talked, had a litter in the night. Do you want to come check them out?"

As strange as it may sound to some, I did reconnect with Rusty's spirit again in the form of a special little golden retriever. This time I didn't hear him speak. I recognized his unmistakable familiar energy, which resonated out to me from one tiny dog in the pile of puppies Auntie Maggie placed in front of me. His energy was like a flag that waved *"Here I am. It's me."*

I am in awe of the way the dream of the wrong mother was validated. First by the sensation of Rusty at the front door, then by the cloud images of angels heralding an arrival, and finally by the phone call from Auntie Maggie. The fact that I had shared everything with my husband as it occurred proved to be invaluable. I might have had a hard time believing the amazing chain of events actually happened if I'd kept everything to myself!

⌐

Kat was having a bout with insomnia when she dreamed that a Scottish ancestor came to her. He explained that for their particular genetic body type, they needed to eat meat, which she already did and loved. But here's the key: he instructed her to eat meat at night so she could sleep. She tried it in real life, and her insomnia vanished!

Dream encounters like this one, in the form of a metaphor, can help us cope with loss and grief.

> The night after our mother died, my sister, who had not been able to be with our mother when she died, experienced a very healing dream. In the dream, a younger version of our mom was driving a car, something that never gave our mother pleasure during her lifetime. The young mom in the dream not only appeared in control, but she was exhilarated, unlike the fearful driver she had been in reality. My sister and mother even had a brief conversation that was positive and joyful. My sister and I interpreted the dream as a message from our mother, letting us know that her journey from life in her physical body to her new state of being had gone well!

WIDE-AWAKE VISIONS

I'd been mulling over a couple of family crises that had been weighing heavily on my heart for some time. Or as my friend Deertrack would say, I was meditating on them and allowing time for the answers to reveal themselves to me. The summer had been traumatic. Our family felt lucky that our granddaughter Ashley was alive after a rollover car accident broke her back. We all wondered what the future had in store for her. I was daydreaming about our family's future as I walked down the hall and, for some reason, glanced up at the skylight. What I saw stopped me in my tracks. The image of a heart had formed at the exact point where the shadow and the light came together. This vision infused me with a strong sense of hope. I was struck by the fact that one side of the heart was dark and the other side was light. For me, the darkness represented the trauma our family had been going through. I felt like this symbol was reminding me how life consists of both darkness and light. And signaling to me that just as night always turns into day, our future was moving into the light.

I think of this image as "the inter-dimensional heart." It was one of those mysterious moments when the Great Mystery reached out with a sign of hope to soothe my soul.

I'm wrapping up this section with this rare vision in order to shed some light on what can occur when we're in that open, relaxed, almost meditative space between dreaming and waking.

Marsha woke up in the middle of the night and lay quietly for a while before she slid out of bed, taking care not to wake her

sleeping husband, and crept down the hall to the kitchen for a glass of water. As she rounded the corner, she saw that the tall schefflera plant they had placed against the wall between the kitchen and the hallway when they moved in seven years earlier appeared to be lit from within. She stopped in her tracks and stood in awe before the plant, trying to take it all in. Her eyes traced the lines of light that were illuminating the veins of the plant.

Marsha describes her experience of this night vision as being allowed to peek into another dimension and experience the photosynthesis in the plant's skeletal structure. "I felt amazed. I knew about photosynthesis, and knew that what I was seeing was the connecting, nourishing process. Experiencing it was like a secret revealed because I was aware and ready to see it. It was a tangible image to me of the connectedness and the process of nourishing. I felt like I was being reminded of the beauty and strength in Nature, the connectedness, the need for being nour-ished and giving nourishment."

I asked Marsha what impact this experience had on her and if there was a larger message for her. "I felt honored to be allowed to experience this hidden dimension. The message for me was to continue my quest for developing awareness . . . the way I had been there just at the right time to observe this incredible process."

Marsha's larger message speaks to all who are opening and expanding their consciousness to welcome the mysteries of our magnificent universe. More hidden dimensions are revealed when we are aware and ready to experience them. Moving into this expanded awareness is easy to do. All it takes is an open heart and mind, a receiver that is turned on, and an intention to pay attention to personal oracles that come our way. Remember, they will be responding to a particular need in your life at the moment, and will translate through a delivery system that will resonate comfortably for you.

Chapter 8

Otherworldly Voices
Messages from the Spirit World

Do not stand at my grave and weep,

I am not there; I do not sleep.

I am a thousand winds that blow,

I am the diamond glints on snow,

I am the sun on ripened grain,

I am the gentle autumn rain.

When you awaken in the morning's hush

I am the swift uplifting rush

Of quiet birds in circling flight.

I am the soft starlight at night.

Do not stand at my grave and cry,

I am not there; I did not die.

—Mary Elizabeth Frye (1932)

Losing someone we love and cherish is one of the greatest challenges in life and one that we will all face at one time or another. Some seek comfort by thinking ahead to the time when they, too, will pass and be reunited in the afterlife with their lost loved one. Others fear that death is a permanent divide—that all ties to their loved one's spirit dissolve into some sort of black hole at the end of their earthly life. Yet stories abound of loved ones communicating from the other side.

In this chapter, we focus on communications from deceased loved ones. These types of experiences assuage grief and bring peace to the heart and soul. Learning about other people's experiences can help us be more open to our experiences and not discount them as "unreal." We celebrate these stories, the people who received messages and shared them, as well as their loved ones from the world of Spirit who made their presence known. As you read these accounts, you may be astonished by the myriad ways people receive messages from loved ones.

THEY'RE PLAYING OUR SONG

Remember my cousin Liz and the song on the radio that announced the time of her friend Steve's death? Well, a decade or so after that event, Liz e-mailed me about another experience with this subject heading: *Another music message in my life.*

On December 14, 2010, my husband Jeff passed away un-expectedly. At least for me it was unexpected. Jeff had been telling me for a couple of months that he wouldn't be coming home from his scheduled surgery. Every time he mentioned dying, I became upset. Maybe he's just teasing me, I thought. As the date approached, he started talking about things he wanted his girls to have when he didn't come home. The day before his surgery, he told me that his brother, Mark, who died a few years earlier, had been visiting him in dreams. I tried to block out his next statement, but it still rings in my ears. "I need to be with Mark," he said. "Please don't be mad."

Jeff went on and on until I finally said, "If you don't want to come home, okay. But if you think I'm going to set up our new business on my own, you're crazy."

Jeff made it through the surgery with flying colors. What had been anticipated to be an eleven-hour surgery only took seven. That night I fell asleep in the chair beside his bed. Around four in the morning a nurse came in to take his vitals.

"Is your husband always this hard to wake up?" she asked.

"No," I said, an alarm sounding inside me. I tried to wake him. When he didn't move, I knew he was gone. The nurse called "Code Blue" and I was led out of the room. As I went out the door, I said, "You, sonofabitch, you knew it, didn't you? You tried to tell me."

I left the hospital that day without my husband. It was the hardest thing I've ever had to do in my life. I lay in bed all night, unable to shut my eyes, missing him. Exhausted, I *finally cried myself to sleep, listening to one of those personalized Internet radio stations on my cell phone. At 4:20 A.M., I woke with a start to a song that was playing. I had never heard it, but these lyrics jumped out at me:*

> *If you think of me*
> *If you miss me once in a while*
> *Then I'll return to you*
> *I'll return and fill that space in your heart.*

I looked at the phone and read: Tracy Chapman's "The Promise." I closed my eyes and fell back to sleep.

The next night around the same time I woke up again to the same song. That's weird, I thought. I knew that on this type of radio station you choose a genre of music and songs play randomly. You can't pick the songs or schedule when they will be played. The station only allows you to go forward or backward by one song. No matter how hard you try, you can't replay a song that played even five or ten minutes ago.

Mystified, I got out of bed and looked up the song on YouTube. A lot of homemade videos came up, many of them made by individuals who put a series of photographs together with "The Promise" playing in the background. I picked one that had a heart-shaped candle with a flame as the first image and punched play. It was beautiful and the images were soothing. As I watched, I almost went into shock. Two minutes and some seconds into the video, the image of Jeff's face with his eyes closed appeared. There was no mistaking it! The person who created the video had included a photo that looked exactly the way Jeff's face had looked at his viewing in his casket.

A few nights later I was driving to a friend's house in the country. I set my phone on the dash of the truck. The dirt road was full of ruts, and the phone kept bouncing around, so I decided to anchor it between the seat and my leg. Suddenly I heard a sound. I glanced down and noticed that my phone was lit up. I picked it up and looked. It was playing the same video of "The Promise." I was startled. I hadn't downloaded the video to my cell. I didn't know how Jeff was pulling this off, but I did know he was signaling me to soothe my heart and to let me know he was present.

Eight months passed. I struggled to develop the business Jeff and I had started just before he died. It was all so new to me that I often became frustrated trying to do everything without him. While driving home after a difficult day, I started to cry and scream at Jeff. I felt abandoned. I needed him to show me that he was still with me, that we were still doing this business together.

My sons Guy and Hunter were at the house that day. Guy is a very spiritual Native American man who can help spirits communicate with us. That evening I told the boys about my earlier rant on Jeff. As we talked, Guy began sweating and clearing his throat. He looked at an area directly over Hunter's shoulder and asked, "Did you hear a voice?" Hunter said no, but held out his arm. The hair on it stood straight up. Guy reached over to the space between himself and Hunter. The hair on his arm stood on end, as well. They told me to come over and feel the air. I did. It felt cold, and the hair on my arm stood up.

We decided to get the tape recorder and record our conversation to see if we could pick up the voice Guy had heard. We turned off the TV, placed the recorder on the coffee table between us, and began talking again about nothing in particular. At one point, our conversation lulled, and Guy whispered to me, "Say something to Jeff."

I whispered back, "I don't know what to say."

"Just tell Jeff you love him."

I quit whispering. "Of course I love him. We all love him and miss him."

The conversation continued for a bit, then we rewound the tape. Hunter put on earphones and began listening. A look of bewilderment crossed his face. He tore off the earphones and passed them around. We all took turns listening. Right after I said, "Of course I love him," you can hear Jeff's voice in the distance saying, "I love you."

Once again there was no mistaking Jeff's presence. He was telling me what I'd asked for earlier in the day. He had not abandoned me. He was still here.

Some might chalk up Liz's messages from her husband to coincidence or wishful thinking. But Liz knows better. She had experience on her side. The personal oracle she received ten years earlier from her friend Steve was unmistakable, since it occurred at the exact time he died. It gave her confidence not to discount messages when they started arriving from her husband.

Liz ended her e-mail with a statement that speaks to our propensity for picking up certain personal oracles. "For you it's clouds; for me it's songs on the radio." True to our Native American ancestry, Liz and I don't limit ourselves; we recognize personal oracle messages in an abundance of other forms. A cardinal serves as a delivery system for Liz's grandfather and my uncle Herb's spirit. Almost everyone in Pretty Prairie, Kansas, watches for Pappy Birds to show up when they need support and comfort. Just like the Reverend Herb Bolinger did when he was alive.

All personal oracle messages translate through a form and frequency that resonates easily with the receiver. No one is restricted to one frequency, such as clouds or technology. Luckily, as transmitters and receivers of universal energy, we are designed to pick up messages in every form imaginable.

GETTING THE CALL

George glanced at the caller ID and answered. "Hey, how've you been?"

The familiar voice of his friend Barry came through loud and clear. *"Great, it's so lovely here."*

George never even thought to ask where Barry was. They lapsed into how long it had been since they'd talked, then one thing led to another, and soon they were reminiscing about their days touring as backup musicians for Cher. George looked at his watch and realized he had to run; he was late for an appointment. Barry promised to phone again.

And he did. But this time Barry didn't waste any time with small talk. He began with a request.

"Could you do me a favor and contact my parents and let them know I'm okay . . . and tell them it's lovely here?"

George was puzzled. Barry and his parents had a great relationship.

"Well, sure, Barry. But where are you? Why don't you just contact your parents yourself?"

The line went silent. "Barry?"

Then the voice on the other end replied. *"I thought you knew. I died in February."*

Chatting on a telephone with a deceased friend would shock most of us, but psychic George Lugo has been communicating with the other side since he was a small child. George now serves as a bridge between worlds. Every day he reconnects loved ones who have passed with those still here in the physical realm. With all that said, George told me that hearing his buddy's voice at the other end of the cell phone, sounding exactly as he did when he was alive, was a new one even for him.

George was curious and dialed the cell phone number Barry had been calling from. Barry's father answered and explained that after his son passed, he continued to maintain the cell phone so he could stay in touch with Barry's friends. George didn't want to share the message from Barry over the phone so he went to tell them in person. They were overjoyed.

The next month Barry called again. This time he asked George to tell his father where to find a piece of paper that his father had been searching for. George again went to the house to deliver the message and help the father search. Sure enough, the piece of paper was exactly where Barry said it would be.

The last time Barry called he asked for a final favor. *"Could you please thank my parents for putting me next to my aunt?"* When he called Barry's parents, they had just returned from a trip where they had placed their son's ashes next to his aunt's.

If you have an experience that seems too far outside the box for your own comfort level, remember George and his friend Barry. George has been communicating with spirits all his life. Even so, mysterious messages from the world of Spirit still surprise him.

⌣

The Stanton sisters add another twist to the idea of mysterious phone messages. See what you think about this one.

Once a month, the two sisters, ages fifty-eight and sixty, have a sleepover. Lindsey and Reese stay up late, munch on decadent foods, watch reruns of favorite TV classics, and reminisce about their childhood. They have a running joke that if the show *Father Knows Best* had been *She Who Must Be Obeyed*, their overbearing mother would have been cast in the leading role.

During a recent slumber party, they talked about the mysterious calls Reese had been receiving. They went like this. Reese would answer the phone, and a woman with a firm voice would say, *"Hi, Reese, this is your mom."* Reese would ask, "Who is this?" The woman would say, *"Reese, this is MOM."* Reese said part of the weirdness was that she used Reese's name but wouldn't tell Reese her name. She just kept insisting, *"It's MOM!"* The woman did tell her the number she was calling. It was Reese's phone number with a different area code, so it appeared to be a matter of the woman misdialing. What intrigued Reese was that the woman always phoned when Reese had been talking about or thinking about her mother. It had happened so many times that she began to wonder what was up between this woman and her own mother.

A few days after their last sleepover, the sisters spoke on the phone. Lindsey mentioned that she was having a will drawn up. The minute the words "having a will drawn up" came out of her mouth, something strange happened. A distorted sound filled the phone line. It sounded hollow and muffled, and underneath the whirring noise, it sounded as if someone was struggling to say something. Think Darth Vader. The sisters tried to talk to each other, but the sound drowned out both of their voices. It was eerie. It didn't sound like any normal voice, even a distorted one. The sisters just listened in shocked silence. They were unable to make out the words, but they did recognize the admonishing tone.

"We couldn't understand it," said Lindsey. "But we felt it was typical of our mother to interrupt with a 'Yes you should,' and 'You better do it right away,' and 'What have you been thinking neglecting that,' et cetera, et cetera. . . . She had a certain tone she used when she really needed to get our attention. We dubbed it the 'Darth Vader Mommy Voice.'" The timing of both events and the distinct way they related to their mother left no doubt in the sisters' minds that their mother was behind it all.

Start listening and comparing notes with friends and family. You may discover that mysterious interconnections like these aren't as unusual as you might think.

Sometimes we want to hear from our loved ones so much that we're afraid to trust those mysterious messages when they do occur.

Gina had been noticing signs that seemed to come from her deceased husband, but she wanted so much for them to be real that she was afraid to trust what was happening. She also didn't want to fool herself by believing his spirit was still close by if it wasn't.

One day she called a friend to help her decipher some signs she'd been receiving. "What I really want to know is that Dan's spirit is still with me." At that exact moment she heard a series of loud thuds. She looked across the room to a tall stack of empty boxes that had been piled in the corner for weeks, just in time to watch them all tumble to the floor. She whispered into the phone, "Oh my gosh, he's right here!" There was no doubt in her mind this time. She asked for what she wanted—to know if Dan was still with her—and Dan answered immediately.

Gina wanted to note, for any skeptics reading this, that the boxes were stacked neatly in the corner. There were no windows or doors open to create a draft. There were no big trucks driving by on the road in front of the house. And there were no earth tremors reported in California that day.

Then there was the time Gina called a Target store and was put on hold. Her mind drifted to Dan and a holiday they'd taken when she was jerked back into the moment. Muzak was playing their song! She listened as the song played all the way through. The moment the song ended, the operator came back on the line. "Hello, is someone helping you?"

As more and more synchronicities occurred, Gina had a harder and harder time chalking them up to chance. The tipping point occurred one day after her shower, when she was in their bedroom getting dressed. A loud clatter startled her. She glanced into the bathroom and noticed one of Dan's socks draped neatly over the side of the tub. It had not been there moments before, when she stepped out of the shower over the side of the tub. The precise placement of the sock was strange, like a flag signaling, *"Hey, come over here."* And so she did.

Gina knew the sock had been stuffed on top of trinkets and mementos from work inside the thank-you mug Dan kept on top of the back of the toilet. She walked over to pick up the sock. Something strange was going on. Beside the tub was the mug, shattered into bits and pieces. Inside the tub lay a message that was arranged as neatly as the sock. One pottery shard had broken into a V shape, and beside it was a long strip of paper. On the pottery shard were the words "THANK YOU." On the paper, "4-BU Dan H."

Tears welled up in Gina's eyes. She remembered what she'd said to him near the end of his long, drawn-out illness when he was cranky and she felt like he was taking her nurturing efforts for granted.

"You know, you could at least say thank you once in a while."

Ever since he passed, she had felt guilty for saying that.

Now, after all this time, she had a perfectly coded thank-you from Dan! His pet name for Gina was Boo. He had even signed his name: Dan H.

A few years later, while missing the sound of his voice, something told Gina; *"Get your old answering machine out . . . right now!"* She didn't hesitate. She retrieved it, dusted it off, and plugged it in. She felt compelled to turn the cassette over and listen. A little voice said, *"You know that tape is twenty years old. There's nothing on it. You erased all of the messages from Dan long ago."* But she ignored the monkey mind chatter and pushed play.

"Hey, Boo, just called to say I love you. Hope you're having a good day."

Years later, messages from Dan continue to arrive whenever

Gina needs them. She accepts them and responds with a heartfelt "Thank you, Dan."

⌒

Carol Anne stopped at a market to pick up a few last-minute items before rushing home to make dinner. She was standing in front of the dairy section, trying to decide which yogurt to buy for her fruit shake the next morning, when she felt something leaning against her shoulder. Without moving her head, she glanced down. There before her eyes was the black and white fabric of a dress she knew well. It was her sister Bonnie's dress, one of her favorites, in fact, and her sister was wearing it. The strange part was that Bonnie had died unexpectedly a few weeks before, at the age of thirty-three. Yet here she was. Carol Anne could even feel her sister's energy, as bubbly as ever.

"I was shocked by her translucent physical presence and afraid that if I moved an inch, I would lose her."

Carol Anne stood perfectly still, not wanting to break their connection. She couldn't take her eyes off Bonnie in the black and white dress. Carol Anne was thinking about how that dress had always looked so darling on her sister when Bonnie's clothes changed! It was as if someone clicked a button. Now she wore another favorite outfit, her green plaid shirt that brought out her tan complexion and big brown eyes.

Carol Anne said the experience was hard to describe. "Her presence felt almost sacred to me. She was fully my sister, yet her body partly blended with my body. She didn't stand totally apart from me—her right side was part of my left side."

Carol Anne never dreamed she would have the opportunity to experience her sister's one-of-a-kind energy again, let alone share some kind of out-of-body hug in a store where they had often shopped together. She hesitated to share what had happened, afraid that a reaction of disbelief might taint her experience. A few days later, Bonnie's brother-in-law, Scott, opened up and recounted a Bonnie "sighting" that he'd had in the days following Bonnie's death.

It had occurred at Carol Anne's house, where the family had gathered after the funeral to reminisce about Bonnie and feast on food that friends and neighbors had brought to express their condolences. Scott had walked into the kitchen to fetch something from the refrigerator. That's when he saw Bonnie standing in a corner of the room. In a flash she disappeared. Scott was reluctant to share his experience because he felt guilty that he had gotten to see Bonnie when no one else had.

There are a jillion reasons why we hesitate to share stories of encountering spirits. We fear that others will think we're crazy. We don't want to contend with a negative reaction. And we don't want others to feel left out of the experience. Sharing our experiences of these mysterious visits, however, especially with supportive individuals, validates those experiences and enables the supernatural to become accepted as the norm.

WINGED MESSENGERS

Beginning to recognize that the spirits of loved ones remain around us is a lot like buying a red car and then noticing how many red cars are out there. Once you start tuning in, you become aware that this type of personal oracle story is everywhere, even on network television.

An account of a mother-and-son reunion aired on ABC's *20/20* on September 9, 2011, in a program commemorating the victims of 9/11 on the tenth anniversary of the attacks. The video began with sixteen-year-old Nick Chirls standing behind the lectern at Catherine Ellen Chirls's memorial service in Brooklyn Heights, New York, recounting memories of his mother. The first time he spoke the word "mother," a bird landed on the right side of his head and settled into his mop of dark hair. It sat there looking content, like it was in its own nest. It was a showstopper. Nick's mood shifted from sadness to amazement and then laughter. He paused, not knowing what to do. Then he gently removed the baby bird from his hair and cradled it for a moment in cupped hands. You can hear the sound of people giggling in the background.

In an interview, Nick described the experience as special, something that couldn't be explained. "I could swear to God there was some sort of recognition. I was just holding this baby sparrow in my hand, and it looked at me and flew away." He went on to say, "There's no doubt in my mind that my mom was there."

At a funeral service I attended, another bird with a personalized message appeared. The bird was sent by Juan, a young man who had lost his battle with cancer. He was signaling to his loved ones that he was nearby.

The large family, all dressed in white, filed in and filled the first four pews of the sanctuary. A large row of windows spanned the entire area behind the pulpit. The mood was somber as a soloist sang "Ave Maria." Without warning, a commotion started in those first four rows. The family started nudging each other and pointing out the windows. Only those nearby could make out their whispers.

"¡Mira! ¡Mira!"

"¡Es Juan! ¡Es Juan!"

They had spotted a sparrow flying in slow motion, taking what seemed like an eternity to make its way from the left to the right side of the sanctuary window.

Later when I mentioned to Juan's mother that the flight of the sparrow reminded me of a Kabuki figure on a stick, she disagreed vehemently.

Then she explained, "No, no. Mexican toy—papier-mâché bird!" The brothers and sisters had been whispering to each other about how the bird moved "like the stick bird we used to play with!"

Notice how this delivery system—the slow-moving bird—was tailor-made to resonate personally with Juan's family to trigger memories of a favorite toy.

FEELING THE PRESENCE OF A LOVED ONE

Let's move away from messenger birds and funerals, and watch how a dear friend of mine showed up days after she passed. I might not have noticed if not for the heads-up from her husband.

Alberto phoned from Italy to deliver the devastating but inevitable news. "I wanted to let you know Annalisa died last night," he said. "But maybe you've already gotten the message from her."

My heart sank. The last time I had talked with my close friend

Annalisa, she had vowed to wait until I could make my way to Milan to be by her side. She said that she had something important to tell me in person. Now she was gone. Her spirit had been willing, but her body needed to shut down.

I hung up the phone and cried. Alberto's words started to play over in my mind. "Maybe you've already gotten the message from her." I wondered, *Did Alberto know something that I didn't? Was Annalisa's spirit trying to reach me?*

The following day Kenneth and I set off to drive from New Mexico back home to Tucson. My antenna was up, ready and eager to receive any message Annalisa might be sending my way. We made our way down the mountain to the mesa where the sky stretched out for miles ahead of us. I began to feel Annalisa's familiar energy, the way it was before she became ill. Her childlike enthusiasm always shone, and on this day I could feel the lightness of her energy and how delighted she was to break free from her body, which had become debilitated by pain.

I scanned the sky. One cloud formation caught my eye. It looked like a child's drawing of a stick figure—make that two stick figures, striding across the sky hand in hand. There was no doubt in my mind this was Annalisa reunited with her father. She had talked about him so much I felt like I knew him. Annalisa never liked to be alone, and now, there she was in the company of her beloved papa.

I snapped a photo to preserve this message from her and always have been glad I did. After it was developed, I spotted a heart that I hadn't noticed while looking at her cloud outline in the sky. Over the years this heart has become her signature, her recognizable mark. Annalisa's heart-autograph has been on every cloud message that has served to keep us connected through the years, and there have been many.

Sometimes I wonder what was so important that she wanted to tell me in person. Other times I feel pretty sure that she wanted to discuss how we would stay in touch after she passed. Ours is one of those bonds that can't be explained. The moment we met, we felt like sisters. We even looked a bit alike. Living on different continents made it impossible for us to spend as much time together as we wished; yet we never needed physical proximity to remain close. When she was alive, Annalisa and I often talked about how easily our spirits remained connected. We imagined our spirits meeting somewhere in the vast network of space spanning the miles that separated us. We're still doing that, only now I send thoughts her way and she sometimes responds with personal oracle messages that resonate through cloud images. She also loves to surprise me with unexpected visits.

Sensing when a loved one's nearby works differently for each of us. For me, it's a very specific feeling. I feel like someone is staring at me—or like someone is nearby but I can't see them. It also helps to keep in mind that loved ones often make their presence known to us in moments when we're thinking or talking about them.

Here are some other clues in case you're wondering how you might recognize your loved one's energy nearby in spirit form. When people are in physical form we tend to identify them by their one-of-a-kind energy, or the way they sit, stand, walk, talk, or even laugh. After a spirit leaves the body, we tune in to what made that person's energy unique and familiar while they were still in physical form. Was she playful? Did he like to tease? Was their energy light or did it have a sense of heaviness to it? Consider how you felt in his or her presence. Annalisa's energy has a sense of love, lightness, intensity, and joy. When my father is present, I feel stability and a tremendously strong stream of love that is directed specifically to me. I feel like I did when he looked at me during his lifetime. His photo is tacked on a bulletin board in front of my computer. Sometimes when I look at his image, I can feel him sending me his stamp of approval.

Don't worry if you can't put your experience into words when it happens to you. When it comes to this kind of thing, words sometimes fail to communicate. That doesn't mean, however, that you won't feel the connection. Trust me, you'll know it when you feel it!

⌣

Francisco Quiroga owned a small dairy ranch near the town of Magdalena in Sonora, Mexico. At six-foot-two, he stood head and shoulders above everyone. His trademark wasn't the denim jeans and white undershirt—everyone wore that—or even the denim jacket he wore on the hottest days of the summer. "Sweat cools me down," he would say. It wasn't even the red bandanna tucked in his pocket like a flag, or his incredibly thick glasses. It was the fact that he had lost an eye in his youth and didn't feel like he needed to hide it. That was Francisco. He was who he was.

As he grew older, the eyesight in his good eye began to fail, and he had a harder time getting around. It slowed him down but it didn't stop him. When he was eighty-eight, his granddaughter Ana Melina invited him to live with her and her family. He agreed to move in but kept his dairy farm. Every morning Francisco slid his old sun-faded cowboy hat on his head and made his way from

Ana Melina's home to his ranch to tend to the cows. Every after-noon at three o'clock he returned home, hung up his cowboy hat, pulled off his muddy boots, and came into the kitchen, where Ana Melina was making dinner. There he sat in his chair and had his coffee.

Theirs was a playful relationship. Ana Melina was a heavy girl and Francisco liked to tease her about her weight. She teased right back. "You smell like a barnyard. Go get in the shower." He was stubborn and protested, "I don't need to be clean. You want to have a huge water bill?"

One morning he awoke and said that he was too tired to go to the ranch, so he stayed home and napped. Around three o'clock he got up, showered, then went into the kitchen and sat in his chair to watch Ana Melina make dinner. Francisco asked for his coffee and dozed in his chair while it was brewing. Ana Melina heard him take a deep breath and asked him if he needed help going to bed. He didn't answer. Francisco had a massive heart attack in his sleep and was gone.

Ana Melina was in charge of the funeral and all other arrangements that needed to be made. As the weeks passed, she cleaned his belongings out of the bedroom and the rest of the house. At three o'clock each day, you could still find her in the kitchen preparing meals for her family. All that was missing was her grandfather.

On the one-year anniversary of Francisco's death, Ana Melina and her mother were in the kitchen making dinner. They were talking about Francisco and his routine when her mother got a puzzled look on her face.

"Do you smell coffee and barnyard? It smells like Francisco's here!"

It was then that Ana Melina realized her grandfather's familiar scent had been with her throughout the entire year at their regular time as she prepared dinner. Her busy life had continued without his physical presence. Like most of us, she had ignored the signs that her loved one gave her to let her know he was still with her.

Now Ana Melina pays attention. When she smells her grandfather's scent and feels his presence, she lights a candle and serves him a cup of coffee. This act of offering Francisco's spirit a cup of coffee and honoring his presence by lighting a candle is seeded in her Hispanic culture. For Hispanics, it's natural for loved ones to remain nearby after the death of the physical body. In some cultures, death is perceived to be the end. In other cultures, death of the physical body signals a new beginning and marks a soul's transition into the world of Spirit, which some of us realize is not separate at all.

When personal oracle messages from loved ones started to reveal themselves to me and illuminate the awe-inspiring structure of our universe, I began to think about that deep-seated feeling I always had—and so many other people have—that I (and they) will never die. Up to that point, I had chalked that feeling up to an unrealistic notion of wishful thinking and denial of the inevitable. Now I look at it as an instinctive knowing. A realistic awareness. The broader perspective of our spirit's journey. We are here on earth for a short time to have a human experience. When our physical body runs out of life force, our spirit slides out, travels through the veil, and continues on. The body of evidence that gives me this assurance is all around each and every one of us. The secret is illuminated each time we tune in and then share our experiences with kindred spirits.

⌐

I was deep in thought one afternoon as Kenneth and I drove past the cemetery at the north edge of Santa Fe, heading for our summer home in Taos. A few years earlier, I had spotted my father's profile hovering above this cemetery, and I was remembering that beautiful experience. In the midst of that memory came a strong urge to call Deertrack. It had been too long since our last phone call. I missed him. I made a mental note to phone him and arrange to get together as soon as we were settled.

That evening we met our daughter Julie and her family at a local restaurant. We hugged hello, and she handed me the front page of the Taos newspaper.

"Did you hear about Deertrack?" she asked, concern spread across her face. I looked at the picture on the newspaper's front page and read:

Richard Deertrack was a man who meant so much to so many. Born in Taos Pueblo in 1930, he fought as a Marine in the Korean War, and was awarded two Purple Hearts. He went on to serve the United States Government and Taos Tribal Government, and was instrumental in legislature to return Blue Lake to the tribe after a long dispute with the Federal and State Governments. He lived in California for a time, serving as Dean of Admissions at Heartwood Institute, and conducted seminars in Native American traditional ways at Esalen Institute, and many other centers of learning throughout America and the world. He attended the Kyoto Water Conference representing the Indigenous voice of North America, and served as Chairman of the Board at the Environmental Law Center in Santa Fe. He gave keynote addresses for the Bioneers in California and New Mexico, and served on the American Health Services for HIV/AIDS. He worked with the FAA and National Parks Service to establish legislation for overflight regulations over National Parks, and in his spare time, read grant applications for federal funds from Native American tribes and organizations.

Richard Deertrack's heart, however, belonged to his beloved Native American Church, where he served as a fourth generation Road Man, conducting services wherever he was called or needed. His mission was to provide a greener, safer and happier world for our children and those to come through the practice of love, faith, charity, and respect. His family of relatives who have gained spiritual insight and growth reach around the globe, and he will be remembered and missed by so many.

Richard R. Deertrack had passed away quietly in his sleep. The graveside service had been held the day before, and his body was buried in the Santa Fe Cemetery. No wonder I had had a strong urge to get in touch with Deertrack when we passed the cemetery. I didn't need to contact Deertrack. He had contacted me!

Remember the lessons from Deertrack that I shared in a previous chapter—about allowing our personal oracles to expand and teach us? Well, that experience occurred a few years after his death during a drive from Taos to Santa Fe. As I mentioned, it was no accident that I didn't have a camera with me that day. Taking a photo of Deertrack's spirit in cloud form would have distracted me from receiving his message. No doubt the reason he appeared

that day was to pass on that information. Still, I always wish that I had a photo of his spirit in the clouds.

That photo opportunity arrived a few days after I received Deertrack's instructions. I was trying to reach his wife, Linda, to deliver a personal message he had given me for her. In addition, I was eager to share the information that he gave me about personal oracles expanding. As I walked through my living room, I felt his energy. Instinctively, I walked to the sliding glass doors, looked past the sagebrush, and scanned the sky. There was Deertrack's profile signaling to me in a cloud. He was looking over his beloved Taos, Mother Earth, and all of those he loved.

Just as I sat with Annalisa's photo after it was developed, I like to sit with this cloud image of Deertrack in spirit and invite him to teach me. I invite you to do the same.

When I delivered Deertrack's message to Linda, she wasn't surprised that he was continuing to send me valuable information from the other side. To this day, she receives messages from her husband like the one in this next story.

Linda Deertrack was kneeling at her husband's grave just as she had done every day of the month since he had passed. There was no headstone yet, and the rich earth blanketing his grave still felt fresh. She noticed a shard of pottery that hadn't been there the previous day. She picked it up, turned it over in her hand, and saw an image of a teepee, a unique and precise symbol of Deertrack's life work. She knew that her beloved husband was letting her know he was still with her.

When Linda returned to the car, her cell phone was flashing a new message. It was the realtor calling to let her know she had an offer on their home. The synchronicity of finding the image of the teepee and then receiving the message from her realtor left no doubt in her mind that her husband continued not only to be around, but to be looking out for her. Their home and land, which were too much for Linda to care for alone, sold to the first person who saw it.

SEEING THE SIGNS

Seeing is believing—or is believing seeing? Actually it's both. When you tune in to your feelings and know what to look for, you never know what you will find hiding in plain sight.

These are just a few accounts of how our loved ones continue to reach out and connect with us from beyond the veil in order to let us know they are there to guide and comfort us or to say thank you for the love and care we gave them. Some even continue to mentor us from beyond.

All right, let's recap and connect the dots regarding what, where, when, and how you might receive your messages from beyond the veil of separation. Pay attention to the following:

- Familiar places (such as the market where Bonnie and Carol Anne shopped, and the kitchen where Francisco spent the late afternoons)
- Animals (birds at a funeral)
- Clouds (Annalisa with her father, Deertrack when I was trying to reach his wife, and Pandora when I was singing "her" song)
- Smells (Cindy's and Wally's fathers, Pandora, and Francisco Quiroga)
- Cell phones (George Lugo's friend and my cousin Liz's husband, Jeff)
- Car radios and tape recorders (my cousin Liz, her friend Steve, and her husband, Jeff)
- Songs (Liz and Gina)
- Mysterious placement of objects (Gina's shifting boxes and the broken mug)
- Coded messages (the thank-you mug and Deertrack's teepee)
- Absolutely everything imaginable

This list of clues is a starting point based on other people's experiences. Remember, the beauty of personal oracles is that they are tailor-made. Your personal oracles will speak to you in a way that is comfortable and familiar, and they will relate to your need at the time. Moreover, when your messages arrive, they will be as unique to you as the loved one who's sending them.

Now, here's when to be on the lookout for messages from loved ones.

- When talking or thinking about a deceased person, or when you have a strong need to hear from the person
- On birthdays and anniversaries
- On the anniversary of the person's passing
- Soon after the person has passed, to let you know he or she has made the transition and is still with you

The trick is not to limit yourself. Remember that loved ones reconnect when we need to hear from them. Keep track of messages from your loved one, even if they are simple hits and cues that don't feel totally clear at the time. Jot down the date, place, time, and anything else about the occurrence that seems important to note. Update your notes as more pieces of the puzzle slide into place over time, like Annalisa's heart that showed up in a photograph and became her signature.

And don't forget to share! There is magic in sharing. Chances are you will be surprised by the stories people share in return. When we have the courage to share with the right individuals, there is validation for all. We start to expand our awareness of the natural order of things. Before long we experience the paranormal and supernatural as simply natural.

Chapter 9

Embracing Personal Oracles
Incorporating Them into
Your Everyday Life

*Another world is not only possible, she is on her
way. On a quiet day, if you listen carefully you can
hear her breathing.*

—ARUNDHATI ROY

Can you believe that there was a time when people thought
the world was flat? They really did! I bring that up because
living without an awareness of everyday personal oracles is
like living in the illusion of a flat world. It is only a matter of time
before the belief that we live in a multidimensional, interconnected universe that is designed to interact with us is the norm.

Everyday oracles change the way we experience our lives.
When we start noticing personal oracles that are hiding in plain
sight, our life becomes more exciting. Everything is bigger, wider,
more expansive than we thought. The life that seemed mundane
and boring fades into the past. And with each personal oracle that

comes our way, the illusion that we are isolated and alone begins to dissolve and disappear into thin air. We heave a collective sigh, knowing we can relax a bit into the strong, capable arms of our ensouled world that has been tuned in to our needs all along.

You have a choice here. You can either open the door to the assistance that is right there, or ignore the knocking hand on the other side, refusing to open it. Life is a rocky journey and sometimes we all get worn out and weary from climbing over the obstacles that keep popping up in our path. The good news is the world is not flat, so you never have to worry about dropping off the edge if you lose your traction. Just keep putting one foot in front of the other and be on the lookout for personal oracles to assist you along your way. Whether you are an exhausted new mom, caught in the midst of a pity party, injured, ill, afraid, looking for moral support, or missing a loved one, personal oracles are there for you. You could be stranded somewhere or in harm's way. You might have more bills than money. It is in these moments precisely that you can experience mysterious arms supporting you—if only you are willing to feel them. Welcome to the world of personal oracles.

In the next few stories, watch as these everyday people recognize how personal oracles are responding to their everyday needs.

While driving to the mall, Hillary allowed herself a pity party. Life had been pitching her curveballs, and she couldn't seem to find the balance to take a healthy swing at them. Or so she thought. She grabbed a tissue from her purse and wiped her eyes. The song on the radio caught her attention. She turned up the volume and listened. The band U2 was singing "Stuck in a Moment."

You've got to get yourself together
You've got stuck in a moment
And now you can't get out of it

Hillary regularly followed the guidance of personal oracles, and often received messages from song lyrics. *Well, I am stuck in a moment*, she thought, *but right now I deserve to feel sorry for myself. This song isn't an oracle. It's just a coincidence.*

She turned into the mall and looked for a parking place near her favorite store. She headed up one row full of cars, then noticed a spot a row over, so she turned down that row. A closer spot appeared, one she hadn't noticed, and she pulled in. Directly in front of her was a large gray pickup with a license plate that shouted to her. The bold black letters on the white background spelled out "No Sniveling."

What else could Hillary do but laugh? The universe had busted her pity party, though it had taken some pretty loud knocking before the door opened. Hillary expressed gratitude for the emotional lift, the reassurance that things weren't as bad as they seemed, the universe's persistence, and the reminder to trust in the guidance of personal oracles.

Then there's my friend Amelia Sheldon, who was no stranger to hard work. She even thrived on the pressures of her job as an editor for a large publishing house in New York City. Nothing, however, had prepared Amelia for the demands of her life as a new mother. Within the first few months of her daughter Raven Faye's birth, she began to have recurring dreams of flat tires.

One day, while she was with her infant daughter in the family car, running errands, she noticed the steering wheel tugging relentlessly to one side. The left front tire was losing air fast. Her flat-tire dreams had become reality. She wondered what Spirit was trying to tell her. She had her "aha" moment the day she and I discussed how metaphoric experiences can offer valuable guidance if we take the time to reflect on them.

"I get it!" she said. "I'm just 'flat tired.'"

After Amelia understood what these personal oracle messages—the dreams and then actually having a flat tire—were telling her on a deeper level, she started giving herself breaks throughout the day instead of pushing ahead so hard.

A nurse and teacher who attended some of my workshops e-mailed me this response to her urgent request from a cloud messenger.

> *Wednesday, when I fell chasing my dog on slick tiles, I sprained my back. I took myself to urgent care, and as I was driving, I kept saying, "I need my guardian angel." I looked up, and Ann—there she was, wings and all. She stayed with me the entire drive. You can't begin to imagine the gift you've given me. Raising awareness to seeing the Blessings and Help around us all the time is critical.*

Dianne was driving along thinking about her deceased husband when she noticed their song, John Lennon's "Woman," playing on the car radio. She smiled when the familiar chorus played "I looove youuu, yeah, yeah, yeah, now and forever," remembering how much her husband had liked to sing along and draw out the words, exaggerating each one for emphasis. While she was listening and remembering, she glanced at the license plate on the car in the next lane. It read BLVNLV. She blinked and looked again. The license plate read like he was texting her. The message was loud and clear. Gene was close by, reminding her to "believe in love," their love.

Signals like these from loved ones who are nearby can come from out of the blue, when we least expect them. Other times they arrive right when we are thinking about that person.

Soraya pulled her coat more tightly around herself as she walked alone in an open field near her home in Nottingham, England. It was the place where she went to try to regain her sense of balance. Even though the death of her seriously ill mother, Victoria, had been inevitable, the empty space her mother left behind sometimes felt overwhelming. This was one of those times when the finality of their separation seemed almost too much for the daughter to bear. Her mind was replaying vignettes of their precious time together when a sudden gust of wind came from nowhere. It swirled around Soraya, embracing her in the warm, familiar energy of her mother. And then her mother was gone. For that one moment, the veil separating the seen from the unseen had parted and reunited mother and daughter on the physical plane. Soraya says she never dreamed she would feel her mother's energy again. But it happened on that magical day.

Somehow Victoria managed to make her presence felt using the wind as her conduit. Soraya hadn't prayed for something like this to occur or even hoped she could reunite with her mother.

This was a mother's spontaneous response to her daughter's need. Luckily, Soraya recognized her mother's familiar energy. It's worth considering that this type of thing happens more often than we realize, but we don't notice or are afraid to trust what is happening.

PERSONAL ORACLES TO THE RESCUE

Sometimes, when we feel like our world is falling in on us, we need to call for help. Other times, our 911 rescue team reaches us before we know to hit the automatic speed dial. The next few stories are fascinating and dramatic accounts of how the universe can come to our rescue in the nick of time.

Laura was heading into town for supplies, but following an impulse, she stopped to check her mailbox. She smiled when she read the return address on the envelope. It was the woman she called her second mother. Inside was a card with the most beautiful guardian angel on the front. The handwritten note read: "Sending love and this guardian angel your way." She placed the card with the photograph of the guardian angel on the dashboard so she could enjoy it while she made the half-hour trip across the mountain and down the winding road.

Her first stop in town was the gas station. As she opened the door, the card blew off the dashboard and landed under the car, just inside her left front tire. She got down on her knees to retrieve her guardian angel and noticed the rubber inside the tire was so worn it looked as if sheer rubber threads were holding it together. The metal threads poking out of it were visible only from this ground-level perspective. If Laura hadn't bent down, she never would have seen how deteriorated the tire was. She glanced over at the other front tire. It was in the same dilapidated condition. Her intuition said, *"Don't even think about going any further on these tires!"* She pulled out her cell phone and located a tire store. Her second stop was Pep Boys for a new set of tires.

The raccoon tracks imprinted in the moist soil looked clear and fresh. Candice turned the four-wheeler and forged a path between trees, over underbrush, keeping as close to the tiny paw prints as possible. She loved spending weekends at their second home near Lake Texoma in southern Oklahoma. It was her way to de-stress from the demands of family and the work week. She had a routine. She'd feed her husband and son lunch, then take off by herself for three hours or so, stocked with water, trail mix, a knife, and matches. Even if cell service had been available, she wouldn't have taken a phone. The only technology she wanted was the four-wheeler.

Being in the woods alone never frightened Candice. The only thing she was afraid of was the pack of wild dogs that roamed the forty-thousand-acre wilderness. Her neighbor had counted nine feral canines running in a group. Even the copperhead snakes that camouflaged themselves in the underbrush and could easily be stepped on didn't worry her as much as the wild dogs. She'd seen their tracks out here before, sometimes right next to the deer, squirrel, and raccoon tracks.

Candice saw a small creek ahead and accelerated. The front wheels, struggling to navigate the deceptively soft, thick mud, made it halfway across and then sank to a halt. Candice peered over the side. The once cylindrical front tire looked like a half-moon. She put the vehicle in reverse. The tires spun and mud flew in every direction. What a mess.

Candice tried everything she could think of to budge the four-wheeler, but the mud would not release its prey. The angle of the sun signaled that it was time to head home. She wouldn't have minded walking back to the house, but she had no idea where she was. While tracking animals, she had crisscrossed this way and that and had totally lost her bearings. She was pretty sure that if she set off on foot she would eventually find her way to the lake or out to a bordering road, but could she do that before dark? And what about the wild dogs? As a former dog trainer, she knew that running into them could spell disaster. Panic began to inch into her.

She sat in the four-wheeler and looked up through the break in the tree canopy, trying to center her emotions. A hawk soared across the hazy blue sky. If only she had a bird's-eye view of the land. The hawk circled. Once. Twice. Candice thought about the game that she and her twelve-year-old son often played on the drive from the city to the lake home. They called it the Hawk Game. Whoever counted the most hawks flying on their side of the car was the winner.

A hawk's beauty and presence had always touched Candice on a deeply spiritual level. She watched the majestic bird glide above her again and thought-spoke a message to the hawk, *"I need your help. Tell my son to come find me. Tell him to take the other four-wheeler and find me. Please guide him to me."*

The hawk circled once more and then again. And then it was gone.

Candice closed her eyes and repeated her request for help like a mantra in her mind, holding it out in front of her like a stick on fire protecting her from danger. She didn't know what else to do except wait and hope that, come dinnertime, her family would note her absence and search for her.

Before an hour had elapsed, the sound of a distant motor thrummed through the trees. Candice sat up in her seat and listened hard. Her first impulse was to yell, but she knew she would never be heard over the sound of the motor. The sound stopped. She turned the key in the ignition and gunned the motor for a moment, hoping to signal whoever it was. Specks of mud hit her back.

She turned off the motor and listened in the silence that followed. The distant motor called again. It sounded like it was moving closer. But then it stopped. Candice fired up the pistons and called back. The conversation continued, each engine speaking to the other, the distance between them closing, until she caught a glimpse of red metal between the trunks of aspens and elms. She jumped to the ground and started waving her arms. Daryn, her son, was driving standing up, heading straight for her, one arm arcing back and forth. Coils of rope and chain were visible.

Wrapping both arms around her young son, Candice said, "You got the message, didn't you?"

"Yeah, Mom, I did."

Together they hooked up the two vehicles, dislodged her four-wheeler, and headed for home, the sound of their motors drowning out the howls of wild dogs.

This event happened more than ten years ago. Candice says that hawks continue to act as personal oracles in her life and in Daryn's. Now an adult, Daryn has had to endure unexpected physical and emotional hardships. Whenever Candice sees a hawk swooping overhead, she knows it's a signal. She sends out a blessing and a prayer for Daryn and, if she can, calls him. Inevitably she discovers that he is facing a particularly difficult challenge and welcomes his mother's support, as well as the support of the universe.

Following is another story of spontaneous timely support. Note the very different form this personal oracle takes.

Kyla pulled out of Tucson just as planned, at six A.M., right after her morning cup of coffee. Thanksgiving was the following day and she was eager to get to her friend's house in Albuquerque, New Mexico, and help with any last-minute preparations and catch up over a glass of wine. She estimated her arrival time to be three o'clock.

Her friend had phoned her the night before to warn her that snow was predicted in Albuquerque and the surrounding Rio Grande Valley. Kyla drove under a clear blue sky until about noon, when clouds started to accumulate. It wasn't long before a light snow began to fall. At first Kyla didn't need to turn on the windshield wipers, but as the flurries turned into flakes and the flakes increased in thickness and population, she flipped them on. Fortunately, the freeway stretched straight in front of her. Snow swirled lightly over the pavement. When she braked to pull off at a rest stop, she felt a slight skid of the rear wheels.

As she pulled back onto the freeway, Kyla decided she'd better proceed at a slower speed, even though she had another hundred miles to go. The snow started to fall heavier. She flipped through radio stations in search of a weather report.

"A blizzard is predicted for the Albuquerque area. Expect it to roll in between five and six o'clock tonight and continue into Thanksgiving Day. For those of you traveling, be cautious. We have reports that the roads are getting slick."

A truck going much too fast passed Kyla, and she felt the back tires slip again on the pavement. *Well, this isn't much fun,* she thought. The wiper blades swished back and forth, back and forth. She didn't have a good feeling and toyed with the idea of stopping for the night and continuing in the morning or even early afternoon.

That's when she noticed an oddly shaped cloud directly in front of her. It looked like a woman with outstretched arms hovering ahead of her in the sky. Something inside her told Kyla to follow the cloud. Maybe she could push through. With both hands on the wheel and concentrating fully on her surroundings, she kept going.

Thirty miles came and went. The cloud remained front and center, never changing shape. She didn't even question how in the world that could happen; she just pushed on.

Now the snow fell heavier and stuck to the ground. Her speedometer pointed to thirty-five miles per hour. The light had diminished, yet she could still see the cloud. Finally she passed a sign. *Welcome to Albuquerque.*

Later that evening, while Kyla and her friend sat by a warm fire, sipping a mellow red wine, the Department of Transportation closed the freeway. The blizzard was in full swing. Wind and snow kept I-40 closed for three days!

On her list of things to be thankful for, Kyla included the flying cloud woman who guided her safely to the home of her friend.

⌐

The next two stories might seem a series of lucky coincidences until you consider them through the paradigm of personal oracles.

Gwen glanced at the clock. Nine P.M. Only one more hour until her shift ended. No customers stood at the gas pumps outside and none roamed the aisles of the small convenience store. Now was her chance to clean the women's restroom. She wanted to make sure to leave on time tonight because she needed to stop at the grocery store before it closed to pick up milk and bread for the morning. She really wanted to get some toothpaste and allergy medicine, too, but at the moment her tight budget couldn't support those purchases. As it was, she was wondering how she could pay the fifty-dollar water bill due in three days.

"Don't panic, not yet," she counseled herself.

The instant Gwen stepped into the restroom, she saw it. A thick red wallet perched on the edge of the porcelain sink. Someone was having a bad night. Gwen opened it and found the Texas driver's license at the top of a neatly stacked row of credit cards with a photo she recognized. It was the woman in the white SUV with Texas license plates who had come inside to use the restroom. When Gwen had said hi, the woman flashed a friendly but distracted smile. "Stephanie Childs," read the driver's license.

Gwen pulled up the corner of a wad of bills and counted. Whoa, there were six fifties and a couple of hundred-dollar bills. She wondered what it would be like to carry so much cash. A small part of her wanted to bolt right then and there and go crazy spending, but it was the small, dreamy part of her. The other part knew what she had to do—hang on to the wallet and wait for

Stephanie to return. Back at the register, she tucked the wallet behind a pile of phone books stacked on a shelf underneath the counter.

Around the same time, Stephanie was nearing a Texas toll-booth. Her three kids, in the back, finally had fallen asleep. For the previous ninety miles, they had argued and laughed and basically taken advantage of the fact that she was driving and couldn't run interference. She had turned the radio on low and was listening to a talk show on the religious station. She passed a sign indicating a tollbooth was just ahead.

Keeping one hand on the wheel, she reached for her purse on the front seat. She rummaged around in the large bag but didn't feel any rectangular object. She pulled the purse onto her lap and tossed makeup, mints, a hairbrush, tissues, and pens onto the passenger seat. Her panic rose as the purse got lighter. No wallet. She swept her hand around the floor as far she could reach. It was night. She had another two hours to drive, tolls to pay, no money, and no ID. Should she scream or cry or both?

"I'm sorry, I can't find my wallet," Stephanie said to the toll-booth attendant. He loaned her his flashlight. She got out and walked around to the passenger side and gave the front seat a good going-over. "I think I left it at the gas station back about twenty miles. Would you mind if I went through and turned around?"

The attendant peered in the car. "Go ahead," he said.

Stephanie felt sick to her stomach. She berated herself for not paying attention. At the gas station, she had filled up the car, then, not wanting to haul three kids out, locked them safely in the vehicle and made a quick dash into the restroom.

"Please, please, please, let someone have turned in the

wallet." What a hassle if it couldn't be found, not to mention the loss of money. Rarely did she carry so much cash. She forced her mind to stay positive and off the path of panic. She visualized a Good Samaritan holding on to the wallet. How would she thank that person? What kind of reward would she offer?

That's when she remembered the talk show. The host had interviewed a guest expert about tipping and what rewards are appropriate. The guest suggested giving a ten percent reward for returning lost money. Suddenly Stephanie had a feeling that someone had found her wallet. Instead of screaming and crying, she wanted to laugh. She felt almost giddy.

Gwen saw Stephanie pull into the filling station and jump out of the car. She heard the beep of the car lock as Stephanie burst through the door. Gwen had already retrieved the wallet and was holding it up in plain sight for Stephanie to see.

"Thank God you have it," said Stephanie. "I was frantic."

Gwen handed it to her and explained where she had found it. She felt just as relieved as Stephanie.

"Here," Stephanie said, unzipping the red leather. "I'd like to give you something."

"Oh goodness, no. I'm just glad I could help out. I'm a mother, too. I know how it goes." She waved her hand in the air as if brushing away the idea.

The next thing Gwen knew, Stephanie had grasped her hand and pushed a folded bill into her palm.

"This is thank you. You saved me so many headaches, I can't tell you."

Gwen looked down and saw the number fifty. She clasped her hand and put it next to her cheek.

"No, thank *you*," she whispered around the lump in her throat. "You can't imagine how much I need this."

Mildred writes that the signs of a Kansas autumn were every-where.

> *Even our budget was heaving that long, slow sigh of relief as the high electricity bills of the hot summer months decreased along with the temperature. I'd been putting off paying the gas bill in order to keep paying the electric bill, but the time had come to turn on the furnace, so I got online and paid my gas bill. The next day I went to work as usual and then ran errands. I arrived home at dusk to find a dis-connect notice from the gas company on my door! I ran to the phone and called the gas company to complain.*
>
> *"How could you shut my gas off? I paid the bill online yesterday!"*
>
> *The voice on the other end was unsympathetic. "Sorry, ma'am, the earliest we can turn your gas back on is to-morrow. That is, if someone can be there to meet the serviceman."*
>
> *At this point things didn't seem to be going my way. It took some juggling to leave work, but I managed. When I arrived home, the serviceman was already hard at work. He stopped what he was doing and walked toward me with a serious look on his face. "You have a gas leak. We'll be replacing the pipes from the street to the house." He wanted me to know that he'd already put a note on my account,*

instructing the billing department not to charge me for the
service disconnect and restoration, since they had to shut
the gas off to do the work anyway.

He also informed me that the gas leak near the street
would have gone unnoticed if they hadn't "accidentally"
turned the gas off. He said that any discarded cigarette or
even a spark from a lawn mower could have set off an
explosion at my house. We had dodged a bullet! So when
the temperature dropped two nights later and we turned
our heater on, we were feeling pretty snug and secure. Oh
yes, and very lucky.

Mildred concluded by saying, "The series of events—the gas being turned off that caused the repairman to come turn it on and discover the gas leak—was truly an act of God." Some might call it luck, coincidence, or even an accident. Whatever we call it, it's clearly another one of those welcome personal oracles that reminds us we're always being helped by hidden hands.

Candice's natural inclination to enlist a hawk in her rescue may inspire you to venture out of the box and consider the telepathic connections that are just waiting to engage with us.

Kyla's cloud angel may inspire you to ask for help when it seems to be nowhere in sight.

The synchronicities of Stephanie's wallet offer hope that when we're doing the best we can, the universe might just have something wonderful up its sleeve. And the gas leak—well, what can I say about those amazing synchronicities!

Each of these individuals had a specific need that was met by her specific *personal* oracle. Such is the characteristic of personal oracles. They are always coming to our rescue and expanding our awareness.

The more we recognize these messages, the more secure we feel, knowing that we're cradled safely within the interconnected web of universal energy.

It's important to keep in mind that personal oracles are never a one-size-fits-all experience. What speaks to you might not speak to me, and vice versa. Each message is always tailored to meet the needs of the specific situation and individual. The key is learning to decode how your personal oracles speak to you.

Take a minute and let your favorite stories pop back into your mind.

- Which ones are most comfortable to you?
- Which ones are most intriguing?
- Do any of them inspire you?
- Do any of them stir memories of your own experiences that you can now relate to through the paradigm of personal oracles?
- Are you intrigued to tune in to discover how the universe is speaking directly to you?

The idea of telepathically connecting with a hawk to deliver an urgent message may be as new to you as it was to me. Learning about Candice's experience opened my mind to the possibilities. As you expand your awareness into other frequencies and dimensions, pay attention to your flashes of insight. Listen to your gut feelings. Don't discount anything as too strange or impossible just because you haven't experienced it for yourself. Stay in your right brain and tune out that left-brain monkey mind chatter.

SPIRIT MADE VISIBLE

In the next few accounts, watch how spirits become visible. These stories come to us from a girl in Texas and some left-brain businesspeople who opened up, stepped out of the box, and welcomed these new dimensions as the natural order of things.

A girl in Texas started noticing the semitransparent spirit-image of a girl standing at the sink in the kitchen. What she didn't know was that other family members were seeing the same young girl, in the same translucent image, also standing at the kitchen sink. For the longest time, nobody mentioned what he or she was seeing.

Private sightings of her mysterious images went on for a few years. Finally, one of the family members opened up and described what she was seeing. It had a domino effect of validation. They never did know who the girl was, or what she was doing there, but they did know they *all* saw her.

Nothing was out of the ordinary the day my husband, Kenneth, reconnected with his father's spirit. He was merely looking into our dog Rusty's eyes as he stroked his head. Then in a flash he became aware of the spirit of his deceased father signaling to him through Rusty's eyes!

Granted, a father's spirit translating through a dog's eyes may sound strange. What is even stranger is when you take into account that the person experiencing it has a very logic-driven engineer brain. No one has ever accused Kenneth of being a "New Ager." Yet his journey with me into the world of everyday personal oracles has allowed him to experience the supernatural for himself. Now he accepts occurrences like this as a matter of course.

I probed deeper to try to determine what this particular experience was like for him. How did he *know* it was his father? Kenneth thought about it for a while and then described it as a familiar look he and his father exchanged when he was alive—an acknowledgment of their unique relationship as father and son. This brief flash of recognition made it possible for Kenneth to welcome and accept the love his father was sending his way.

⌐

A high-profile businesswoman was plagued with so many speed camera tickets that she started taking alternate routes to avoid the cameras. Not a day went by that she didn't dread going to court to face the consequences. She even rented a small apartment in another state for the summer in an attempt to postpone the inevitable. But when her court date finally arrived, you'll never guess what happened. The records of her speeding tickets were nowhere to be found!

What does this businesswoman think happened to the court's missing records?

"My dad always rides with me in my car," she said. "I'm sure he took care of it for me."

Her father has been deceased for years.

⌣

Julianne turned her car into the driveway and started up the hill to the house when something caught her eye.

"It's Willie's spirit!"

A few weeks earlier, she had cradled their much-loved family dog in her arms as he passed. Now she watched the unmistakable translucent image of their big black Labrador race across the front of their house directly above the area where he was buried. Willie's long legs looked even longer as he glided through the air. Although she couldn't see his running buddies, she had a very strong feeling that he wasn't alone.

⌣

When Bruce moved into his first house in Tucson, he started experiencing inexplicable phenomena. Forks kept showing up everywhere, except in the kitchen drawer where they belonged! He found forks scattered in random places around the house. Some forks even ended up on top of a bookcase! He was attending a party at a friend's house when someone pointed out that he had a fork sticking out of his back pocket.

I shared this story with a friend who said, "Oh, sure. When I lived in that area, mysterious stuff like that happened all the time. Everyone knows Native Americans used to live there, and they're always making their spirits visible in one form or another. They just like to let us know they're around."

I shared this story with another woman who added another

intriguing piece to the puzzle. "In Native American symbolism, a fork or a V in nature is a symbolic gateway or path into the spirit realm." By making this symbolic leap from a fork in nature to a piece of cutlery, the spirits used what was available to let Bruce know they were still around.

⌐

A few weeks after her husband's death, Mrs. Lung started having recurring dreams of her husband sitting in a classroom. The idea of him continuing his studies seemed natural because he'd spent a large part of his life on earth as a student. She didn't give the dreams much more thought until later that year, when a psychic told her that her husband was taking classes. Now she was intrigued. The third time the dreams came up, she was taken aback. This time a work associate of Chen Lung's told her about a dream that he'd had. In his dream Chen was taking classes!

When we trust our gut and know what to be on the lookout for, our connection with these other frequencies and dimensions expands naturally. Then before we know it, we start to recognize that supernatural occurrences are simply the result of connecting with a different energy frequency. And we emerge from the limited perspective of a three-dimensional world—that flat world that can make us feel isolated and alone.

In these final accounts of mystical connections, watch as more spirits become visible. The first personal oracle was no coincidence or accident. I reached out to Pandora through the veil that separates us, and she reached back.

Part German shepherd, part Australian sheepdog, and part wolf, Pandora was truly one of a kind. One minute she would be howling with the coyotes, and the next minute she would be snuggling beside me. Whoever named her at the shelter was spot-on. Like her Greek namesake, the first mortal woman made by Zeus and endowed with a gift from each god, Pandora possessed the gifts of beauty, persuasion, a love of music, that amazing howling voice, and especially curiosity. When we first met, she wouldn't, or couldn't, stand on her own, and would eat only when fed by hand. No doubt she was weak from not eating, and she was giving up on life. Her tenderhearted spirit had been broken by abuse. Still, my husband and I knew the moment we saw her that she was part of our family, so we took her home and loved her back to life.

Now that she has passed, I sorely miss having her physical presence by my side. I continue the routine of our morning walks, which we took together for eleven wonderful years. I sing the same songs I sang to her all her life, to let her know I'm thinking about her and wishing she was still right here beside me: "Pandora, where are you? You're such a little girl. Pandora, we love you, you make our life a whirl . . . wind." I alternate that song with my version of the theme song from PBS's *Mister Rogers' Neighborhood*.

Some days I can sense Pandora's spirit leaping and prancing happily along beside me. Other days I not only sense her presence nearby, but spot her image in the clouds as well. As I approached our driveway on one particular day, her spirit-presence in a cloud image was absolutely breathtaking. I ran inside, grabbed my camera, and snapped this photo.

Note: Her image in the clouds is a reverse image of the photo I took of her in our driveway a few days before she died.

If you don't see Pandora's image in the clouds, try this exercise:

Focus on the photo of her in physical form. Then focus on the cloud image. Locate the bright white line that runs diagonally. That is her front leg. Above her leg is a small dark circle—that is her nose at the end of her snout. Below her nose a light white line outlines her mouth. Rest your gaze on the cloud image for a while and let her entire face emerge.

I never stopped to think that by singing her songs with the intention of sending a message to her, I had upgraded the energy of my morning walk from a routine ritual to a sacred ritual. My intention to let Pandora know how much I miss her engaged the channels of communication between our parallel dimensions, and Pandora responded in kind.

Toning our psychic muscles and refining our intuition can be as simple as tuning in to energy frequencies that reveal themselves in everyday routines and rituals. Routine without intention is like going through life on automatic pilot. Try adding a specific intention to an everyday routine and see what surprises await you.

Another time, Pandora helped me expand my expectation of how she might reveal her presence to me. I'd grown accustomed to Pandora replicating herself in a cloud version of her physical image, so that's what I was on the lookout for. My awareness broadened unexpectedly the day there were no clouds in the sky. I remember making an offhand comment to Kenneth, "Looks like Pandora won't be showing herself in any clouds today." As we continued walking, however, her presence became palpable, and I went on alert to see if there was some other way she might be trying to communicate with us. We had walked a hundred yards or so, when off in the distant sky, I noticed a tiny puff of cloud. It seemed to materialize out of nowhere and then quickly formed the shape of a heart. In a flash, I understood Pandora was signaling us. The heart remained long enough for me to point it out to Kenneth, and for us to voice our agreement that it looked like Pandora was reaching out to us through it. Then the tiny cloud disappeared.

Photographing cloud images is another good way to deepen our awareness and help us tune in to spirits as they become visible. Having a photograph to look at also allows messages to expand and crystallize, like Annalisa's heart that became her spirit-signature.

I've always been a camera bug, so photographing cloud images that catch my eye is second nature to me. It all began with clouds that caught my attention and mirrored timely messages back to me. Some cloud images triggered a thought-message. These images evolved into a cloud-speak game that I played with friends. We would sit around a table, gazing at cloud photographs and giving them titles. We identified a flying pig to symbolize POSSIBILITIES, a cloud face in CONTEMPLATION, an Asian dancing figure we titled JOY, a cloud face that looked like it was blowing we titled WINDS OF CHANGE; even a pair of those HELPING HANDS showed up! You name it, and if you look often and long enough, you can see it in the clouds. This cloud game with friends took on a new life when I realized the images and concepts functioned as personal oracle messages.

Phyllis and Fred were a married couple who loved to play this game. I remember sitting with them at my worktable and listening to Phyllis try to convince Fred that what she saw was *the* correct interpretation of an image. However, it didn't take her long to realize that there is never just one cloud interpretation. Or that one interpretation isn't necessarily better than another. Like life, cloud interpretation isn't restricted to only this way or that way being correct. Everything expands; everything's this *and* that *and* that *and* that. . . . It's fascinating to see how an image resonates so differently with each of us.

I often hear people say, "That's not what I see." Precisely. Each of us experiences life through our own movie camera. Every perspective is perfect and unique. When it comes to personal oracles, we see what we need to see—when we need to see it!

It didn't surprise me when Phyllis's spirit showed up in cloud form a few days after she passed. I was pulling up my driveway when I noticed an unmistakable cloud image of Phyllis hovering just above our driveway. She looked like she was gesturing toward Phoenix, where her family was gathered at the bedside of their youngest daughter, who was in the final stages of pancreatic cancer.

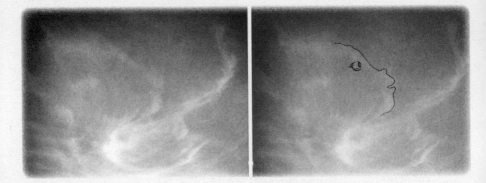

"If you stay right there, I'll photograph you," I said. "Just let me run inside and get my camera."

Phyllis always loved a good party and made it known that when she passed, she didn't want a traditional funeral. She preferred that her friends and family celebrate her life with a margarita party. That's just what we did. The night before her party I had a flash of insight regarding what Phyllis had been signaling through her cloud form. Phyllis had a unique way of talking about her death, like a child anticipating a great adventure. She referred to death as "going bye-bye." So amid margaritas and balloons and toasts to Phyllis's grand new adventure, I handed out copies of her cloud photograph to everyone to take home with them. They all agreed: Phyllis was waving bye-bye!

Phyllis's message in the clouds seems to have at least three interpretations that all link together.

- Phyllis waving bye-bye.
- Phyllis gesturing toward her family gathered in Phoenix.

• And, if you look closely, you may see Phyllis cradling a
  swaddled baby in her arms. The babe represents her
  youngest daughter, Linda, who passed a few days later.

I am particularly blessed and honored to have encountered
the spirits that revealed themselves in the next two cloud images.
I believe that I'm their steward, and my charge is to share them
with people all around the world.

I had been standing on the sky deck of our home, enjoying
the early evening when I felt a familiar benevolent energy all
around me. I could feel it resonating from one particular part of

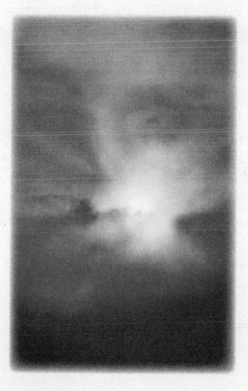

the sky. I looked to that area and saw the faint image of a face, but I wasn't sure what it was. The energy was intense and comforting, though not specifically identifiable. The image remained steadfast, so I retrieved my camera from inside and snapped a photo. When the film was developed, the photo took my breath away. What I had captured looked like and felt like an image of the Divine Mystery we call God revealing itself through the clouds.

This astonishing photo is the result of trusting the unknown and responding to a sense of presence.

⌐

In this last story, you can connect the dots as this invisible moving sidewalk put me in the right place at the right time to witness this not-so-hidden spirit in a cloud. And to think it all started with an energy shift.

It didn't seem to matter that terrorists were wreaking havoc in Kosovo and Serbia and even crossing the Adriatic Sea to threaten every port in the Mediterranean.

As far as the cruise line was concerned, our reservation was set in stone. I told them my reason for canceling was the danger in the area, but that wasn't the real reason. The idea of being pampered and indulged when people nearby were being tortured and maimed felt totally inappropriate to me.

As the departure date approached, it looked like our only alternative was to be a no-show. Then one morning while in meditation I felt the negative energy that had been surrounding the trip shift 180 degrees. Suddenly I felt compelled to go. So off Kenneth and I went to cruise the Mediterranean with friends.

The year was 1999. Cities around the world were sprucing up

to welcome the new millennium, and Rome was no exception. Our day in the Eternal City dawned clear and mild. Kenneth and I ignored warnings to avoid large public gatherings and headed straight for St. Peter's Square, where Pope John Paul II was holding a special Mass. Some might assume I'm Catholic, since I chose to attend a Mass rather than visit ancient sites, but no. Nor do I speak Italian or Latin, so I knew I wouldn't understand a word that was being said. I *thought* my reason for going was to see this particular pope. This man of faith, who was living his highest spirit purpose, had always intrigued me. I respected his reputation for inclusiveness and wondered how it would feel to be in his presence.

Security was tight, but we made our way through the scanning areas and located two folding chairs where we sat to wait with thousands of other people. Men in black robes took turns speaking from a lectern underneath a red canopy flanked by restoration scaffolding. It was a bright sunny day, and with no pope yet in sight, I watched the steady stream of pilgrims from all over the world who continued to file in. A dozen rows ahead of us, a nurse and a nun sat close together, escaping the intense rays of sunshine under the shade of an umbrella.

After a while I began to feel a strong sense of protection. My attention shifted to an expansive cloud image hovering directly over the seating area. As I gazed more deeply into the cloud, the image of a face with a beard emerged. This face, in turn, appeared to be gazing down on the gathering. I was fascinated. This cloud was not like most clouds that move across the sky and then morph into different shapes. This cloud held its space. Five, ten, twenty minutes passed and this cloud still held fast. The benevolent energy became so intense that I glanced around, expecting everyone to be pointing up at the cloud. No one but me was looking up at the sky! The crowd's energy was as focused on earthly matters as mine was focused on this cloud and its astounding energy. I wanted to jump up and down and point to the sky ... or something. But I decided to take photos instead.

Pope John Paul finally arrived in his Popemobile and spoke to the crowd. My interest remained tethered to the mysterious cloud and the energy still surrounding me. It was clear that some mystical connection had occurred; I just didn't know what it was. I became curious about the monk in the portrait that hung in a prominent place on the scaffolding beside the stage so I snapped this photo.

Back on board the ship, I left the film to be developed, went back to the cabin, kicked off my shoes, and turned on the TV to check in with CNN world news. Instead of the standard reports on terrorist activities that I expected to see, the network was running a special program about Padre Pio, the saint known for his association with paranormal phenomena. The host and some clergymen talked about the stigmata: the wounds in Padre Pio's hands that seeped blood and smelled of roses. They also discussed some of the miracles he was known for during his life. I learned that the Mass at St. Peter's Square that day was Padre Pio's beatification ceremony—the final step in a process to declare him a saint.

It was a lightbulb moment. This saint-to-be was actually present at his own ceremony, and I bet that I had photos to prove it! Eagerly I placed the photo of the portrait beside the cloud image and confirmed my hunch. Both were three-quarter views of the same face.

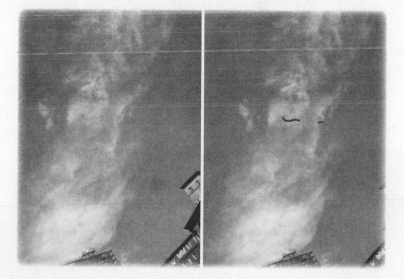

I immediately started sharing the photos with friends on the cruise. Some saw the image immediately, but once I made another copy and ran a line underneath his closed eyelids, everyone was able to see it.

God does have a sense of humor. In some quirky way, the genius of revealing Padre Pio to a non-Catholic makes this experience even more authentic, since I had no idea what a beatification ceremony was or even who Padre Pio was at the time!

Padre Pio's one-of-a-kind energy and image in the clouds is a magnificent gift that expanded my horizons and continues to enrich and inspire my life, just as it does for millions of others around the world, as his renown continues to grow. Some two hundred monuments are dedicated to him. There are thousands of prayer groups around the world that draw inspiration from him. His faithful admirers include Protestants, Buddhists, and Hindus.

Stories of Padre Pio like the ones below allow us to glimpse beyond the restrictions of the three-dimensional world. Accounts of his bi-locating—that is, showing up in two places at a time— shatter the boundaries of time and space. His ability to levitate and read minds, along with his well-documented premonitions, continue to open our perception to the possibility of dimensions that expand beyond the norm.

The sky-related events are especially fascinating to me. During World War II, Allied pilots were sent to bomb San Giovanni Rotondo in Italy, but were stopped by the appearance of a "monk" standing in the air with his arms outstretched, imploring the pilots not to bomb but to return to their base, which they did. As it turned out, the Germans weren't even in San Giovanni when the bombs would have been dropped. In his book *Padre Pio: The*

True Story, Bernard Ruffin writes: "There are pilots who swore that they had sighted a figure in the sky, sometimes normal size, sometimes gigantic, usually in the form of a monk or a priest. The sightings were too frequent and the reports came from too many sources to be totally discounted. Several people from Foggia, where thousands were killed during air raids, said that a bomb, falling into a room where they had huddled, landed near a photograph of Padre Pio. They claimed that when it exploded, it 'burst like a bubble.' Others reported that while the bombs were raining down upon the city, they cried, 'Padre Pio, you have to save us.' And while they were speaking, a bomb fell into their midst but did not explode." Accounts of Padre Pio being sighted at the Vatican while he was still in San Giovanni Rotondo add to the mystery of his ability to bi-locate.

Another intriguing account, about the miraculous healing of a worker named Giovanni Savino, who had lost an eye that later materialized under his bandages after Padre Pio visited him, brings to mind Rachel's miraculous healing after she prayed with the chaplain.

The wonders that surround us are beyond our wildest imaginations. Once our antenna is up and we learn to connect the dots, we notice that these spirit signposts and mysterious bulletins and mystical messages keep coming our way—always when we need them the most. Soothing our soul, guiding our way, illuminating our path, and making visible our connection with everything around us as well as those beyond the veil. That's when the illusion of being isolated and alone begins to dissolve.

12 TIPS FOR TUNING IN TO
PERSONAL ORACLES

1. Open your heart and mind and welcome the unknown.
2. In your mind's eye, imagine yourself connected to the higher frequency of light energy that is working for your highest good.
3. Set your intention and invite the world of spirit to communicate with you.
4. See yourself as a successful receiver of messages.
5. Invite universal spirit to show you the way.
6. Engage your psychic antenna—then pay attention to what you pick up.
7. Tune in to the elegant nuance of your intuition.
8. Keep in mind that the world is filled with metaphors and emerging shapes. Notice what attracts your attention and how you are drawn to it.
9. Remember, your personal oracles are always tailored specifically to you and to your particular needs at any given moment.
10. Tame that monkey mind chatter! Ignore your monkey mind if it tries to plant doubt or draw you into a dialogue. It's just trying to deflect your attention from your inner knowing.
11. Use sticky notes and shoe boxes, journals, or e-files to document and store your personal oracles and cultivate your intuition.

When your intuition sends you an important message, write it down while it's still fresh in your mind. When that nudge says,

"Something special is happening here," grab a notebook, sticky note, iPad, phone, or computer and record it. This is how you get to know and expand your intuition. Plus, it prevents you from believing in such monkey mind chatter as *"That didn't really happen," "You're just imagining it," "It's not logical."*

The sticky-note shoe-box method is a friendly alternative if you're technically challenged or not one to write in a journal. You don't have to use an actual shoe box; it can be any box or container in which you store those experiences you want to remember. Maybe you've written notes on a napkin in a restaurant or scribbled on the back of a photo or torn off a sticky note from a pad in your desk or that you carry with you. Just plunk those pieces of paper in the box for future reference.

A shoe box also is an ideal place to store photographs of your mysterious cloud messages, or any other forms that come your way. When you see an image that you want to remember but don't have a camera handy, pick up a pen or pencil and draw it, then add it to your shoe box collection. My shoe box contains photographs, notes, quotes, newspaper clippings, a feather that drifted to the ground right in front of my feet, and a multitude of other solved and unsolved mysteries. You'll be amazed at how fast your stockpile of personal oracle experiences grows. Reviewing them can be enlightening. The meaning of some messages crystallizes over time. What you didn't understand then, you may understand now, or later.

And in case you're wondering what to do when you fill up your shoe box, there are always drawers!

12. Remember to share your experiences with others; this validates and expands everyone's awareness.

This book is a compilation of everyday personal oracles that are available to all. They're ours for the taking. Whether you're an old hand at living outside the restricted three-dimensional world, or just peeking to see what's out there, stop and reflect on the accounts you've just read.

Which ones give you pause, pique your curiosity, stir memories of your own experiences, speak personally to you, validate something you've been wondering about, illuminate how interconnected everything is?

I hope I've shed some light on how your personal oracles may be speaking to you. When you close this book I hope you are excited about everything that is in your corner, working for your highest good every day.

If you're heading out to gather your own body of experiences, remember: when it comes to interpreting personal oracles, there is no right way or wrong way. Messages come in every form imaginable.

And—don't ever worry about a pop quiz—you have all your own answers.

Just try it. I promise that those strong, indelible interconnections are there, have always been there, and always will be there, guiding and supporting you all the way.

Expect the Unexpected— and You Won't Be Disappointed

One bright February morning in Arizona, a local labyrinth guide, Mary Anne Carpo, came to walk our garden labyrinth with me to honor her eightieth birthday. I looped a camera around my neck to record her special occasion. Mary Anne led the way while I followed some distance behind, whispering the words and tune of this labyrinth song to myself as we walked.

There is a path to the mystery

And as I walk it reveals to me
The truth, the deep, the way
I trust the path of the mystery
That as I walk it's revealed to me
The truth, the deep, the way
Hey ah hey ah hey ah ho

Hey ah hey ah hey ah ho
Hey ah hey ah hey ah ho
Show me the way through the mystery
Transmute my darkness

Help me see

The truth, the deep, the way
Great mother of the mystery
Bless my soul

Illumine me

To the truth, the deep, the way
Hey ah hey ah hey ah ho
Hey ah hey ah hey ah ho
Hey ah hey ah hey ah ho

I focused on the words and the crunch of my moccasins as I placed one foot in front of the other on the well-worn gravel path that leads to the center, a repository for silent prayers, secret hopes, and dreams, and back out again. Countless times I had walked this ancient path of transformation that cradled my sorrows, and in perfect time, they were offered back to me again healed and whole.

On this day, ten years after the death of my father's body, as Mary Anne and I trod this ancient path of mystery together, I was thinking of my father. My heart was open and I felt grateful for all he taught me, and how he continues to teach me from beyond the veil. Right then, I became aware of my father's spirit smiling down on us. I paused for a moment and pointed the camera to the specific area of the sky where I felt his familiar energy, *knowing* that his image was there in the clouds.

When our labyrinth walk ended, I explained why I had stopped to take the photo.

Mary Anne said, "I hope he shows up in your photo."

I told her that I knew he would.

 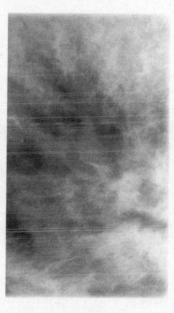

My father,
Earl Bolinger, in life.

His spirit resonating
through cloud form.

Oliver Wendell Holmes could have been talking about the miraculous effect personal oracles have on our life when he wrote: "A mind that is stretched by a new experience can never go back to its old dimensions."

Sometimes we can feel like we are caught in a maze. We feel

confused and blocked and don't know which way to turn. And then there are times when life just keeps tossing us curveballs. A maze is a complex puzzle with twists and turns and dead ends. But mazes and labyrinths are quite differ-

ent. A maze is a left-brain intellectual exercise; a labyrinth is a right-brain spiritual one. Even if you don't think of yourself as spiritual per se, remember, you are not a human having a spiritual experience. We are all spirits having a human experience here on earth.

Labyrinths are like life. If you look at one from a distance, it looks confusing, perhaps even overwhelming. When you move in closer, you can see that the twists and turns form one single pathway. You cannot get lost. There are no dead ends. Labyrinths are easy to navigate. All you need to do is place one foot in front of the other, open yourself to embrace the mysteries of life, and continue moving forward.

The labyrinth is an archetype for our life journey that we can walk or, in the case of this finger labyrinth, trace with our finger. As we travel this symbolic mystical path, we create a sacred space in a place that rebalances our energy and helps us along our way. The guidance and support we need awaits us at every twist and turn. Our life becomes a living labyrinth when we walk our path with an open heart and a spirit of curiosity for discovering the mysteries that lie ahead.

When you close this book, remember that wherever you go,

I'm cheering you on, and the universe has your back. And don't forget, your personal oracles are hiding in plain sight, waiting for you to notice them as you continue on the ever-expanding cycle of opening to the path of mystery and discovery.

Namaste.

Tips, Tools, and Exercises for Tuning In to Your Personal Oracles

When you walk across the fields with your mind
pure and holy then from all the stones, and all
growing things, and all animals, the sparks of
their soul come out and cling to you and they are
purified and become a holy fire in you.

—ANCIENT HASIDIC SAYING

L et's take a look at some tried-and-true methods that have been used throughout time to quiet the mind, raise energy frequency, and expand consciousness. See which exercises resonate with you and give them a try. Maybe it's only one, or maybe it's all of them. Don't worry about choosing "the right" one, because there isn't one. And don't put expectations on yourself. As mentioned earlier in the book, there won't be a pop quiz; no one will be checking to see if you're doing any of these exercises in the proper way. There is no proper way. Do it your way. Setting your intention sets everything in motion. The one thing that is helpful is to pay attention. You never know when personal oracles will speak to you.

LABYRINTHS

You may already be a fan of labyrinths as a form of deepening your awareness and centering your physical, emotional, mental, and spiritual bodies. If so, you know just how powerful they can be. If not, you're probably wondering what a labyrinth is and why you should consider journeying its pathway.

In short, a labyrinth is an ancient symbol that combines the imagery of a circle with a spiral and creates an interactive, purposeful path. It serves as an archetype for our life journey, one that we can walk on foot or, in the case of a finger labyrinth, trace with a finger. As we travel this symbolic, mystical path, we create a sacred space that helps rebalance us on all levels. This simple, contemplative pathway is a tool that can quiet the mind and open the heart.

It's important to understand that labyrinths and mazes are quite different. A maze is a complex puzzle with choices of paths and directions. A labyrinth has one single pathway. There are no dead ends, so you can't get lost. A maze is an intellectual exercise; a labyrinth is a spiritual one.

Labyrinths are easy to navigate. All you have to do is set your intention, place one foot in front of the other, and continue moving forward along a path that meanders back and forth and delivers you to a center point, then brings you back out again to your original starting point. There are no choices to make once you enter the labyrinth. The mind is free to concentrate on the journey. Psychologists report that the repeated twists in the labyrinth stimulate both the left and the right hemispheres of the brain, a phenomenon that walkers report brings a sense of balance and well-being to their journey.

Nicholas Halpin, counselor at Dundee University in Scotland, refers to labyrinths as "spiritual tuning forks." He has observed that "the more people who walk it at one time, the more energy there is, which is very tangible in terms of the warm, tingling feeling I get from it. And even when I come off and sit near it, I can feel the energy pulsating off the labyrinth in waves—a clear demonstration of spiritual energy." Halpin goes on to say that in his experience, the majority of people walk the labyrinth to de stress. "They probably lead very busy lives and therefore deliberately walk in a measured way in order to slow themselves down." Halpin, however, finds it more beneficial to walk the labyrinth rather quickly. "It fires me up—in particular my creativity. I once walked the labyrinth at a rate of knots, having a meeting to attend in twenty minutes. I wheeled around it and came out with a complete poem in my head!"

That is the beauty of labyrinths. Just as in life, what we receive along our journey depends on what we need at the time.

Different forms of labyrinth designs are used all around the world as contemplative pathways. Some date back thousands of years. There are turf labyrinths in the UK and Germany, usually found on village greens. Hundreds of examples of stone labyrinths exist in Scandinavia, while ancient labyrinths abound in India, Greece, Egypt, and even North and South America. Think of any country, in fact, and there's a good chance you can find labyrinths there. I know many individuals who travel around the

world and seek out labyrinths in each new city they visit and make
an effort to walk the path.

In the last few decades, there has been a revival of interest in
the labyrinth and a return to this form of "slow cooking" contemplation. During the last fifteen years in the United States
alone, more than two hundred labyrinths have been built in hos-
pitals. At the National Naval Medical Center in Bethesda, Mary-
land, the labyrinth is being used to help veterans with PTSD.
They are also being built in universities, public parks, and schools.
Thousands of people have constructed them in their backyards or
painted them on their basement floor. You can even purchase a
portable canvas labyrinth that can be rolled up when not in use.

Labyrinths are used to enhance the lives of those who choose
to walk the path in a spirit of openness and reverence for life.
Buddhists, Christians, Agnostics, and others with deeply felt
beliefs that don't click neatly into one category or another find
comfort, peace, and often clarification as they walk the way of the
labyrinth. By using this simple pathway to quiet the mind and
open the heart, we reconnect to seen and unseen dimensions. The
labyrinth brings us full circle and enables us to embrace the wisdom of the ancient ones who came before us.

MEDITATION

The goal of traditional meditation is to quiet the analytical mind
and enter a state of receptivity and balance. As we learn to relax
into this stillness, our heart opens and we reconnect with the
essence of our being.

To help us embrace mys-
tifying messages that flow
through our own inner wisdom and the divine mystery,
the following exercises acti-
vate four of our seven
chakras—the Solar Plexus,
the Heart, the Throat, and the
Third Eye.

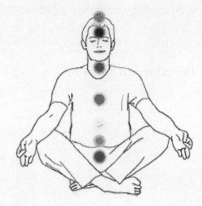

What are chakras? They
are force centers considered
to be the focal points for the reception and transmission of
energies.

In the first three exercises, you will place your hand on
your belly. Why the belly? According to the ancient chakra system, the belly is where the solar plexus/navel center is located.
This center relates to the rational mind. By placing your right
hand on the belly and your left hand on a specific energy center,
you create an avenue that links these centers in the body
with the rational mind. By doing this, the perception associated
with that energy center flows into the rational mind. There,
the mind expands that perception and releases any restricted
thinking.

Before you begin each meditation, take a deep breath. As you
exhale, see yourself releasing the cares and concerns of your day.
Now take a second deep breath. This time as you exhale, see this
breath carrying away anything left hanging on. On your third
and last deep breath, inhale deeply, and as you exhale, bring
yourself and all of your energy into the moment.

Connecting your heart and mind

The heart chakra is associated with emotional wisdom.

- Place your left hand on your heart, then place your right hand on your belly.
- Inhale deeply and slowly and then exhale that breath fully and slowly.
- In your mind's eye, watch your breath flowing easily from your heart to your belly and back again and again.
- As you breathe, notice the rhythm of your breath connecting your heart and mind.
- Continue breathing this way until the energy feels complete.

Integrating your left brain and right brain

The throat chakra is associated with abstract and conceptual wisdom.

- Place your left hand on your throat and your right hand on your belly.
- Inhale deeply and slowly and then exhale that breath fully and slowly.
- In your mind's eye, watch your breath flowing easily from your throat to your belly and back again and again.
- As you breathe in and out, notice the rhythm of your breath connecting your abstract mind and your rational mind.

- Continue breathing this way until the energy feels complete.

Activating your intuition

The forehead (third eye) is associated with intuition.

- Place your left hand on your forehead (your third eye), then place your right hand on your belly.
- Inhale deeply and slowly and then exhale that breath fully and slowly.
- In your mind's eye, watch your breath flowing easily from your third eye to your belly and back again and again.
- As you breathe, notice the rhythm of your breath as it opens your third eye.
- Continue breathing this way until the energy feels complete.

The next four meditations help us tune in to the elements of earth, air, water, and fire.

Opening and connecting to Mother Earth

Lie on your belly on a soft spot on the ground and place a small pillow under your head. Turn your head to the side if you like. Relax completely into the support of the earth, allowing as much of your body to be in contact with the earth as possible.

When your body is comfortable and cozied up to the earth, focus on your breath. Inhale long, deep breaths, and then exhale slowly. As you breathe in, imagine that you are drawing the earth's energy into your body. Bring this energy into each part of your body. Remember the diagram of the seven chakra centers and let the energy of the earth bathe and fill each one. Or simply allow the earth energy to flow to each part of your body. Trust your body wisdom to direct the energy flow where it's needed.

As you allow the natural life force of the earth to flow into you, meditate on qualities that you seek in your life, such as stability, peace, wholeness, calmness, and centeredness. Feel these qualities become a part of you and absorb them into your being.

Continue to lie still until your connection with the energy feels complete, and you feel like sitting up. Before you do, you may want to give Mother Earth a hug and express your gratitude to her for always supporting you and sharing her energy with you.

Air meditation

Before you begin this meditation, become aware of the air that surrounds your body. Inhale and experience this refreshing air as it fills your lungs. Hold the air gently in your lungs, and then, with gratitude, release it back out into the world, bringing your awareness to the oneness of all. Be mindful that each time you inhale and exhale, you are dancing an intimate dance with all life.

- Lie on your back in a comfortable position in a hammock, a lounge chair, or on the ground.
- Look up into the sky. Gaze into the blue expanse and feel your mind becoming, as the Tibetans say, as "vast as

the sky" and opening to encompass all possibilities, all of creation.

· Feel the total freedom of the sky's limitlessness, and experience your being expanding to become vast— without limit and totally free.

· Close your eyes and allow yourself to drift in this limit-lessness of being.

· When you feel like opening your eyes, express your gratitude for the limitlessness of being, then return your focus to earth.

Water meditation

In his revolutionary book *The Hidden Messages in Water*, Japanese scientist Masaru Emoto documents in photos how molecules of water are affected by our thoughts, words, and feelings. He details experiments showing that the vibration of emotions alters the molecules of water and explains that: "The entire universe is in a state of vibration and each thing generates its own frequency."

As we continue to sharpen our senses, keep in mind that everything generates its own frequency, from cells to emotions to all that is in nature, on this planet, and even beyond. Go into this water meditation with the intention of opening yourself to receive all positive vibratory messages.

Now, to begin:

· Find a comfortable spot near a body of water—a lake, stream, river, ocean, pool, or fountain. Watch the move-ment of the water—the eternal flow.

- *Notice* the light reflecting on the water. See yourself merging with the shadows, ripples, waves, eddies, and the many subtle changing colors.
- *Experience* the qualities of the water—fluid, flowing, changing, adapting.
- *Allow* the water to carry you into another state of being, into your feelings, into the mysterious waters of your intuitive self.
- *Embrace* the comfort and security within these mysterious waters.
- *Recognize* the familiar sound, touch, feel of this wisdom of your intuitive self.
- *Know* it is integral to your very being.
- *Trust* that this wisdom is always available to you.
- Remain beside the water until you feel like it is time for you to leave.
- Go in gratitude, taking to heart all that you experienced there.

Fire gazing

Fire gazing is an activity that's popular around the world and dates back thousands of years. You may want to acknowledge your ancestors who gazed into a fire and even invite them to accompany you as you continue to fine-tune your sixth sense.

- First set your intention.
- There may be something specific that you would like the fire to answer for you. Think it or say it out loud.

- If you would like to connect to someone on the other side, state that, as well.
- Open your heart.
- Invite the fire to speak to you.
- Focus on the motion of the flames.
- Embrace the comfort and security of the energy with which you connect.
- Recognize the familiar sound, touch, feel of this wisdom of your intuitive self.
- Know it is integral to your very being.
- Trust that this wisdom is always available to you.
- Remain by the fire until you feel like it is time for you to leave.
- Go in gratitude, taking to heart all that you experienced there.

MANTRAS

You may be familiar with mantras as a popular way to reprogram thoughts and behavior. If not, here's the powerful first step. Set your intention and then carefully choose the words for what you want to achieve. You might want to say something like this: "I am a finely tuned energy receiver. I notice personal oracles that guide me every day."

- Write your mantra on a piece of paper.
- Stick it up on your bathroom mirror or on your daily calendar. Make it the wallpaper for the screen on your

computer or cell phone. Choose a place where you can read the words frequently.

- Speak the words out loud.
- Repeat them in your mind throughout the day.
- Repeat them during meditations.

The repetitive process of a mantra reprograms a mind-set and works like a fine-tuning mechanism. When my monkey mind starts chattering, I find it helpful to chant a mantra to pull out of its control. If you like to make up spontaneous songs and ditties like I do, you can add a melody to your mantra. Set the words to a catchy cadence and sing it to yourself. A smile is almost guaranteed. Here's one I made up when Parkinson's disease was giving my dad a tough time. It became our mantra, which I sang and chanted to him over and over and over. "All you can do is the best you can do, and that's all."

MUDRAS

If the Sanskrit word *mudra* is new to you, I'll bet the images aren't. The familiar image of two hands with palms together pointing upward is a universal gesture of prayer or respect. Sacred gestures such as this date back centuries and were used by cultures around the world to connect the practitioner with the divine and cosmic energy. Let's add the mudra of wisdom to the tool kit you are creating to help you sharpen your senses. What does the mudra of wisdom do? This mudra stimulates the mind and clears your access to higher knowledge and wisdom.

The mudra of wisdom can help resolve any conflict you are facing by helping you see beyond your individual problems and into the bigger picture and higher meaning of any situation. This is a very powerful mudra, but it does require devoted practice.

To use the mudra of wisdom:

- Sit with a straight back on the floor or a chair.
- Curl your thumbs into your palms with your last three fingers over them, leaving your index fingers extended.
- Keep your shoulders down and relaxed, but raise your elbows out to either side.
- Bring your curled hands in front of your chest and hook the index fingers together, right palm facing the ground, left palm facing your chest, forearms parallel to the floor.
- BREATHE—LONG, DEEP, and SLOW breaths.
- Hold the mudra for three to eleven minutes.
- Relax and sit still.

Do this mudra every day for three weeks and it will help you identify the answers to your questions and the purpose behind your life's challenges more easily.

(Mudra information is from Sabrina Mesko's book *Healing Mudras: Yoga for Your Hands*.)

It's easy to incorporate mudras into everyday life with the intention of recognizing and strengthening the connection between yourself and the energy of the universe. Here's a playful exercise that isn't a mudra but is fun to do with friends and gives you an immediate "read" on each other's energy fields.

- Place your open hand or hands within a couple of inches or so of your friend's hands.
- Hold still.
- Focus your attention on your hands. Do you feel the energy of your auras?
- Move your hands closer together and farther apart. What do you feel?

CHANTING

Chanting is an ancient practice that raises vibratory levels. Simply stated, chanting works through the frequency of sound and increases the magnitude of energy with repetition. Chanting with intention can transform negative energy into positive energy. Chanting certain phrases over and over again shifts the vibration and effects change in mind, body, and spirit. Chanting can quiet the mind, open the heart, and lift your spirit to a higher state of consciousness.

In his book *Ancient Teachings for Beginners*, Douglas De Long explains the mechanics of how chanting works and then instructs us how to chant using the word "MAY."

This chant affects the crown chakra greatly and the third eye chakra or energy center to a lesser degree. The crown chakra is located at the top of the head and is linked on a physical level to the pituitary gland.

When intoned properly, this special chant or sound will send a vibration deep within the head where the pineal gland is situated. This stimulates the gland and surrounding areas of the brain. As this happens the crown chakra will become "activated" and open up. This allows higher vibrations of energy to enter into the crown chakra, the body and the human energy field or aura. This energy is also referred to as chi or universal energy and exists all around you. It is in the air that you breathe and the water that you drink. A brief description of this chanting exercise follows. The sound to use is MAY as in the month.

Before you begin, take a deep breath in and hold it for about five seconds. Then exhale slowly and evenly through your mouth or nose. This is your choice. Repeat this breathing technique two more times. It is important that the deep breathing is done a total of three times. This allows some of this chi or universal energy to be absorbed into the lungs and ultimately the whole body via the circulatory system. This ensures that the brain waves slow down, your auric field around you expands and brightens, and you feel more relaxed. This is necessary in order to receive the full benefits of performing the May chant.

Now, take in another deep breath and hold it for a few seconds. Then, as you exhale out your mouth intone the sound M-A-A-A-Y-Y-Y until all your breath has been expelled. Let the pitch of your voice rise and fall a little as you do this. Take in a second deep breath, hold it once more for a bit and then repeat the chant. Intone the chant a third and final time. Once completed, just relax for a few moments.

One of the effects of this exercise is a feeling of "tingles" on the top of the head where the crown chakra is located. This is a sign that the crown energy center is opening up. It

is starting to receive higher vibrations of universal energy
from the heavenly fields above. Also, it is an indication that
neurons are firing in the cerebrum of the brain, creating
new pathways to other areas within. The cerebrum is the
major mass of the human brain. Some of your psychic abil-
ities are stored within this part of your brain.

Try it for yourself and see what happens. A great thing about chanting is that you can chant anytime and anywhere—in the car, in the shower, on a walk in the park. Chant alone or in a group. I'm part of a global chanting group that meets once a week to direct this transformative energy out into the world. To learn more about global chanting or to find a group you can chant with in your area, Google "global chanting." If there's not a group in your area, maybe you and your friends could start one.

FORMAL RITUAL

A formal ritual is an exercise or series of actions designed to unite the body, mind, emotions, and spirit. Rituals can be private or shared. Following are some basic ideas for designing a ritual for the purpose of uniting your essence with unseen forces and frequencies:

- Set your intention. It might be sharpening your senses, deepening your relationship with the Divine, healing the earth, healing yourself, seeking strength, gaining a deeper understanding of your purpose in the world, or any other objective you may have.

- Select a location. It could be a place in nature, a room in your home, or even your desk at work.
- If you plan to repeat the ritual on a regular basis, remember the value of using the same space over and over in order to tap into the energy that builds in that space.
- If you're not going to use the same place again, it's respectful to release the energy you created back to the universe once your ritual is complete.
- Create the level of privacy you desire. It may be as simple as closing a door or imagining a protective circle around you and your space. You can also create a sacred circle by surrounding your space with lighted candles.
- If you feel awkward or silly when you begin, try to let that go. Remember that this is a personal ritual that you are designing exclusively for yourself.
- Make each part of your ritual meaningful.
- Your ritual can be performed in a spirit of joy and/or reverence.
- Choose ritual items that have special significance for you, such as flowers, candles, incense, crystals, stones, pictures or photos, food or drink. In my ritual, I include a lighted candle, sage, or incense. In the Native American tradition, smoke is used to connect with Spirit.
- Words are powerful tools and may be all you need for your ritual.
- You may use your own written words, or favorite poems, quotations, songs, or chants by others.
- When speaking each word, focus on its meaning.

- When using songs or chants, tune in to the sounds and vibratory energy you are creating.
- When all is in readiness, sit quietly and tune in.
- You may want to end your ritual with a mantra or prayer as an expression of gratitude.

When your ritual is over, sit quietly and tune in again to your feelings. What did you experience during the ritual? How do you feel now that it is over? Make notes of anything that is useful to remember. Know that your energy will go deeper and wider each time you perform your ritual. Keep in mind that there's no correct or incorrect way to tune in. It's all about decoding your own unique process.

Lois McCrystal shared this saying that always seems like one of the ultimate truths. "This is my way, what is your way? The way doesn't exist." When we truly embrace that reality, we can dismiss the internal critic that measures everything we do against someone else's expectations.

⌒

As you begin to explore the exercises presented above, bear in mind the experience of my friend. He said that the deep connection he feels with the universe "didn't happen overnight, it evolved over time." As he explained, "The first time I sat beside a flowing stream, I experienced a sense of peace. Then as time went by, the process of tuning in to water just evolved and expanded naturally." This is his method for releasing emotions into water. "I release a specific emotion, thought, or problem into the water and then watch as it washes away. I imagine it being carried downstream and out of sight, then making its way through the process of purifying and cleansing. In due course, it flows into the ocean, where it transforms to pure water that evaporates into the clouds, which in turn release it back into the atmosphere, where it is free to return to earth." In his mind's eye, he sees himself flowing into this natural cycle and becoming a tiny piece in the magnificent web of interconnections that flow unceasingly between everything in the universe.

He ended by saying, "Reading about other people's experiences can open the door, but stepping through that door and having your firsthand experiences transforms theory into knowing."

Savor the experiences. Savor the knowing.

Acknowledgments

It's worth noting that all of the right people came along, at precisely the right time, to support this book.

I appreciate each one of you more than you will ever know.

My heartfelt thanks . . .

To my gifted editor, Sara Carder, and publisher, Joel Fotinos, for recognizing and believing in this book. To Sara's editorial assistant, Joanna Ng, and the talented team of behind-the-scenes experts at Tarcher/Penguin for their care and craftsmanship. And to Tarcher/Penguin for giving the personal oracles message a home base with big strong wings to fly out into the world.

To Lynn Wiese Sneyd, my exceptional publicist, first line editor, kindred spirit, for convincing me that information delivered in a memorable story stays with us forever, for writing that extraordinary book proposal, and for connecting me with Claire Gerus.

To my esteemed agent, Claire Gerus, for sharing her expertise gleaned through years of working on the other side of the desk in the New York publishing world. For helping Lynn and me craft a table of contents that makes personal oracles jump off the page right into the reader's heart. And for aiming so high that we caught the interest of some of the most highly regarded publishers in the business.

To Amelia Sheldon for her belief in my vision. For serving as the gateway into the publishing world. For working with me during the embryonic stage when my vision of gifts from the universe expanded and deepened, and the term "personal oracles" was born. For our friendship, which has expanded to embrace both of our families. And for connecting me with Lynn Wiese Sneyd!

To Kathy Colletti, my treasured friend and technical-support person in all of my projects that involve photographs. Special thanks for always being just a phone call or e-mail away. For sharing her ability to work with all the photos I take on the fly as events transpire. And for introducing me to Amelia Sheldon!

To Liza Wiemer, author of *Extraordinary Guidance*, for bringing me back from the brink of self-publishing with her words "Wait—don't self-publish. Your book is going to sell to a major publisher!"

To my long-term friend Lisa Thiel for being my consultant on topics that deal with ancient wisdom. And for sharing her artistic skills on another project that is dear to my heart, the Cloud Speak Personal Oracles Book and Cards.

To Donna Fontanarose Rabuck, sister of my soul, for reading through each and every incarnation of this work and journeying with me as the message deepened and expanded over the span of fifteen years.

To all of my sisters of the sacred feminine, for listening with open hearts and always supporting my vision.

To my dear friend Dawn Cole, for being right all along when she said, "This needs to be a how-to book!"

To Clinton Hartmann, for contributing information on how he incorporates his finely tuned right- and left-brain functions.

To all of my friends who cheered me on, and those who voiced their doubts. Each and every one of you played an important part in this journey.

To all of you who shared your story—your contributions are invaluable.

To my family, whose belief in me never wavered. I appreciate all of your encouragement, support, and understanding. I am blessed to be part of a family that shares my perspective. You made the journey so much easier. Special hugs to Aunt Evie, for impressing on me at a very young age the importance of trusting my intuition.

To my husband, Kenneth, for going behind my back in the pet shop that day. Thanks to him, we did take that little puppy with an agenda home.

And . . . to Rusty . . . my father . . . Padre Pio . . . Deertrack . . . Annalisa . . . Phyllis . . . Pandora . . . and all spirits no longer in physical form that continue to expand my awareness of our amazing interconnected universe.

References

Chapter 1. Personal Oracles: Portals into Hidden Dimensions

Old Apache storyteller (epigraph): Joseph Campbell, *The Hero's Journey: Joseph Campbell on His Life and Work.*

Cleve Backster lie detector test on dracaena: Peter Tompkins and Christopher Bird, *The Secret Life of Plants: A Fascinating Account of the Physical, Emotional, and Spiritual Relations Between Plants and Man.*

Animal sightings reference guide: Ted Andrews, *Animal Speak: The Spiritual & Magical Powers of Creatures Great & Small.*

Neladoracht (Druid/Celtic term for cloud divination): *The World Atlas of Divination*, consultant editor John Matthews.

Oracle of Zeus at Dodona and Oracle of Apollo at Delphi: Dianne Skafte, *Listening to the Oracle: The Ancient Art of Finding Guidance in the Signs and Symbols All Around Us.*

Socrates and the Oracle at Delphi: Diogenes Laertius, *Lives and Opinions of Eminent Philosophers*, trans. R. D. Hicks.

Socrates Cafés: Christopher Phillips, *Socrates Café: A Fresh Taste of Philosophy.*

Hawk in a dream that saved a baby's life: Bobby Lake-Thom, *Spirits of the Earth: A Guide to Native American Nature Symbols, Stories, and Ceremonies.*

Hawaiian elder Nana Veary: Anne Wilson Schaef, *Native Wisdom for White Minds: Daily Reflections Inspired by the Native Peoples of the World*; Nana Veary, *Change We Must: My Spiritual Journey.*

Turkey as a sign to Prince Abdullah of Saudi Arabia: George W. Bush, *Decision Points.*

Hindu perspective on a unified field of pure consciousness: Margaret Stutley, *Hinduism*; Michael Talbot, *The Holographic Universe.*

Confucius: Danielle and Oliver Föllmi, *Awakenings: Asian Wisdom for Every Day.*

Quantum physics and the matrix of interconnections between everything in the universe: Gregg Braden, *The Divine Matrix: Bridging Time, Space, Miracles, and Belief.*

Dream weave: Jamie Sams, *Dancing the Dream: The Seven Sacred Paths of Human Transformation.*

Dreamtime: Chris H. Hardy, *The Sacred Network: Megaliths, Cathedrals, Ley Lines, and the Power of Shared Consciousness*; Robert Lawlor, *Voices of the First Day: Awakening in the Aboriginal Dreamtime.*

REFERENCES

Songlines: Bruce Chatwin, *The Songlines*; Robert Lawlor, *Voices of the First Day: Awakening in the Aboriginal Dreamtime*.

Australian Aboriginal elder Aunt Millie Boyd: Anne Wilson Schaef, *Native Wisdom for White Minds: Daily Reflections Inspired by the Native Peoples of the World*.

Leylines: David Cowan and Chris Arnold, *Ley Lines and Earth Energies: A Groundbreaking Exploration of the Earth's Natural Energy and How It Affects Our Health*; Chris H. Hardy, *The Sacred Network: Megaliths, Cathedrals, Ley Lines, and the Power of Shared Consciousness*; Robert Lawlor, *Voices of the First Day: Awakening in the Aboriginal Dreamtime*.

Vortexes: Pete A. Sanders, Jr., *Scientific Vortex Information: How to Easily Understand, Find, and Tap Vortex Energy in Sedona and Wherever You Travel!*; Richard Sutphen, *Sedona: Psychic Energy Vortexes*.

Chapter 2. How Personal Oracles Work: Conduits, Mirrors, and More

Holograms: Michael Talbot, *The Holographic Universe*.

Synchronicities (meaningful coincidences): C. G. Jung, *Memories, Dreams, Reflections*, ed. Aniela Jaffé, trans. Richard and Clara Winston.

Serendipity as "helping hands": Joseph Campbell, *The Hero with a Thousand Faces* (from *The Collected Works of Joseph Campbell*).

Chapter 3. Everyone Has Personal Oracles

Robert the Bruce and the spider: Tom B. Leonard and Joanna Strong, *A Treasury of Hero Stories*.

Isaac Newton: David Berlinski, *Newton's Gift: How Sir Isaac Newton Unlocked the System of the World*; Michael White, *Isaac Newton: The Last Sorcerer*.

Mahatma Gandhi: Mark Shepard, *Mahatma Gandhi and His Myths: Civil Disobedience, Nonviolence, and Satyagraha in the Real World*.

Wayne Dyer's account of the butterfly: Wayne W. Dyer, *Inspiration: Your Ultimate Calling*.

Byron Pitts's story: Byron Pitts, "Overcoming Obstacles," *Guideposts*, http://www.guide-posts.org/inspirational-stories/inspiring-story-byron-pitts-overcomes-obstacles-find-success?page=0,0.

Chapter 4. What Speaks to You? Clouds, Cledons, and Everything in Between

Chief Letakos-Lesa: *The Indians' Book: An Offering by the American Indians of Indian Lore, Musical and Narrative, to Form a Record of the Songs and Legends of Their Race*.

Justin Rollins's story: Kimberly Launier, "Not Photoshopped: Beam of Light Shines on Fallen Soldier's Miracle Dog." http://abcnews.go.com/blogs/headlines/2011/11/not-photoshopped-beam-of-light-shines-on-fallen-soldiers-miracle-dog.

Universal symbols: David Fontana, *The Secret Language of Symbols: A Visual Key to Symbols and Their Meanings*.

Numerology: Ted Andrews, *Animal Speak: The Spiritual & Magical Powers of Creatures Great & Small*.

Legend of ravens at the Tower of London: http://www.hrp.org.uk/TowerOfLondon/stories/theravens.

REFERENCES

Chapter 6. Personal Oracles as Healing Tools: How They Heal and Empower You

"My little bunny" story: Allan J. Hamilton, *The Scalpel and the Soul: Encounters with Surgery, the Supernatural, and the Healing Power of Hope.*

Spiritual medicine: Jamie Sams and David Carson, *Medicine Cards: The Discovery of Power Through the Ways of Animals.*

Flashes of insight: Christiane Northrup, *Women's Bodies, Women's Wisdom: Creating Physical and Emotional Health and Healing*; Deepak Chopra, *Perfect Health: The Complete Mind/Body Guide.*

"Stroke of luck": David Servan-Schreiber, *Anticancer: A New Way of Life.*

"The primitive brain": Michael Gershon, *The Second Brain: A Groundbreaking New Understanding of Nervous Disorders of the Stomach and Intestines.*

Chapter 7. Crinkles in Time: Dreams and Visions

Paul McCartney's dreamed melody for "Yesterday": "Five Dream Discoveries," June 10, 2009, http://news.bbc.co.uk/2/hi/uk_news/magazine/8092029.stm.

Crinkle in time: Alex and the bullet that saved his life: Dean Radin, Colleen Rae, and Ray Hyman, "Is There a Sixth Sense?" *Psychology Today*, July 1, 2000, http://www.psychologytoday.com/articles/200007/is-there-sixth-sense.

Crinkle in time: Lynn Mesrobian-Darmon's story: Lori Weiss, "It Ain't Over Till It's Over: Her Psychic Abilities Saved Her Daughter's Life," *The Huffington Post*, April 25, 2012, http://www.huffingtonpost.com/2012/04/23/it-aint-over-till-its-over-psychicmother_n_1446146.html.

Lisa Hopper's recurring dreams and humanitarian aid: Lisa M. Hopper, *In the Wake of a Dream.*

Chapter 8. Otherworldly Voices: Messages from the Spirit World

Mother-and-son reunion, with a bird landing on the son's head: http://www.youtube.com/watch?v=wwPohaMlvoQ.

Chapter 9. Embracing Personal Oracles: Incorporating Them into Your Everyday Life

Padre Pio and his miracles: C. Bernard Ruffin, *Padre Pio: The True Story*; Brother Francis Mary, F.I., ed., *Padre Pio: The Wonder Worker.*

Additional Resources:

Books from Ann's Personal Library

Ancient Wisdom

Ted Andrews, *Simplified Qabala Magic*
Mary Dean Atwood, *Spirit Healing: Native American Magic & Medicine*
Charlotte Berney, *Fundamentals of Hawaiian Mysticism*
Doug Boyd, *Rolling Thunder*
Joseph Epes Brown, *The Spiritual Legacy of the American Indians*
Gregory Cajete, *Native Science: Natural Laws of Interdependence*
Douglas De Long, *Ancient Teachings for Beginners*
Sam D. Gill and Irene F. Sullivan, *Dictionary of Native American Mythology*
Thomas E. Mails, *Secret Native American Pathways: A Guide to Inner Peace*
Jamie Sams, *Dancing the Dream: The Seven Sacred Paths of Human Transformation*
Andre and Lynette Singer, *Divine Magic: The World of the Supernatural*
James A. Swan, *Sacred Places: How the Living Earth Seeks Our Friendship*
Andrea Wansbury, *Birds: Divine Messengers: Transform Your Life with Their Guidance and Wisdom*

Earth Energies

Bruce Chatwin, *The Songlines*
David Hatcher Childress, *Anti-Gravity & the World Grid*
Chris H. Hardy, *The Sacred Network: Megaliths, Cathedrals, Ley Lines, and the Power of Shared Consciousness*

Chanting

Ted Andrews, *Sacred Sounds: Transformation Through Music & Word*

Dreams

Lisa M. Hopper, *In the Wake of a Dream*
Leon Nacson, *A Stream of Dreams: The Ultimate Dream Decoder for the 21st Century*

William Willoya and Vinson Brown, *Warriors of the Rainbow: Strange and Prophetic Dreams of the Indian Peoples*

Dreamtime

Robert Lawlor, *Voices of the First Day: Awakening in the Aboriginal Dreamtime*

Extrasensory Perception

The Boy Who Saw True, with introduction, afterword, and notes by Cyril Scott
Dawn Baumann Brunke, *Animal Voices: Telepathic Communication in the Web of Life*
Rupert Sheldrake, *Dogs That Know When Their Owners Are Coming Home: And Other Unexplained Powers of Animals*
Liza M. Wiemer, *Extraordinary Guidance: How to Connect with Your Spiritual Guides*
Machaelle Small Wright, *Behaving As If the God in All Life Mattered*

Health

Jeanne Achterberg, *Imagery in Healing: Shamanism and Modern Medicine*
Thorwald Dethlefsen and Rüdiger Dahlke, *The Healing Power of Illness: The Meaning of Symptoms & How to Interpret Them*
Allan J. Hamilton, *The Scalpel and the Soul: Encounters with Surgery, the Supernatural, and the Healing Power of Hope*
Louise L. Hay, *Heal Your Body: The Mental Causes for Physical Illness and the Metaphysical Way to Overcome Them*
David Servan-Schreiber, *Anticancer: A New Way of Life*
O. Carl Simonton, Stephanie Matthews-Simonton, and James L. Creighton, *Getting Well Again: A Step-by-Step, Self-Help Guide to Overcoming Cancer for Patients and Their Families*
Liz Simpson, *The Healing Energies of Earth*

The Human Chakra System

Anodea Judith and Selene Vega, *The Sevenfold Journey: Reclaiming Mind, Body & Spirit Through the Chakras*
Karla McLaren, *Your Aura and Your Chakras: The Owner's Manual*

Interpreting Symbols

Ted Andrews, *Animal Speak: The Spiritual & Magical Powers of Creatures Great & Small*
Ted Andrews, *Nature-Speak: Signs, Omens & Messages in Nature*
J. E. Cirlot, *A Dictionary of Symbols*
Maril Crabtree, *Sacred Feathers: The Power of One Feather to Change Your Life*
Maril Crabtree, *Sacred Stones: How the Power of the Earth Can Change Your Life*
Bobby Lake-Thom, *Spirits of the Earth: A Guide to Native American Nature Symbols, Stories, and Ceremonies*
Sabrina Mesko, *Healing Mudras: Yoga for Your Hands*
Adele Nozedar, *The Element Encyclopedia of Secret Signs and Symbols: The Ultimate A–Z Guide from Alchemy to the Zodiac*
Barbara G. Walker, *The Woman's Dictionary of Symbols and Sacred Objects*
The World Atlas of Divination, consultant editor John Matthews

Labyrinths

Liz Simpson, *The Magic of Labyrinths: Following Your Path, Finding Your Center*
Melissa Gayle West, *Exploring the Labyrinth: A Guide for Healing and Spiritual Growth*

Padre Pio

Renzo Allegri, *Padre Pio: Man of Hope*
C. Bernard Ruffin, *Padre Pio: The True Story*

Science

Cleve Backster, *Primary Perception: Biocommunication with Plants, Living Foods, and Human Cells*
Gregg Braden, *The Divine Matrix: Bridging Time, Space, Miracles, and Belief*
Gregg Braden, *The Spontaneous Healing of Belief: Shattering the Paradigm of False Limits*
Masaru Emoto, *The Hidden Messages in Water*
Masaru Emoto, *The Secret Life of Water*
Bruce H. Lipton, *The Biology of Belief: Unleashing the Power of Consciousness, Matter & Miracles*
James A. Swan, *Nature as Teacher and Healer: How to Reawaken Your Connection with Nature*
James A. Swan, *Sacred Places: How the Living Earth Seeks Our Friendship*
Michael Talbot, *The Holographic Universe: A Remarkable New Theory of Reality That Explains the Paranormal Abilities of the Mind, the Latest Frontiers of Physics and the Unsolved Riddles of Brain and Body*
Jill Bolte Taylor, *My Stroke of Insight: A Brain Scientist's Personal Journey*
Peter Tompkins and Christopher Bird, *The Secret Life of Plants: A Fascinating Account of the Physical, Emotional, and Spiritual Relations Between Plants and Man*
Gary Zukav, *The Dancing Wu Li Masters: An Overview of the New Physics*

"Gangaji is one of the smartest, clearest, and most poetic spiritual leaders of our time. Her writing in *Hidden Treasure* is compassionate, transparent, generous, and ruthless. The mere reading of only a few of her words brings me home to the truth of who I am, in seconds."

—ALANIS MORISSETTE, Grammy Award–winning singer and songwriter

978-0 39916-053-0 • $15.95

""Much more than another 'dream book.' . . . A creative, hopeful, constructive approach to life."

—RICHARD WOODS, O.P., PH.D., associate professor of pastoral studies, Loyola University

978-1-58542-754-3 • $16.95

If you enjoyed this book, visit

www.tarcherbooks.com

and sign up for Tarcher's e-newsletter to receive
special offers, giveaway promotions, and
information on hot upcoming releases.

**TARCHER
PENGUIN**

Great Lives Begin with Great Ideas

New at **www.tarcherbooks.com**
and **www.penguin.com/tarchertalks**:

TARCHER
TALKS

Tarcher Talks, an online video series featuring
interviews with bestselling authors on everything from creativity and prosperity to 2012
and Freemasonry

If you would like to place a bulk order
of this book, call 1-800-847-5515.

31901056168232